FIX-IT and FORGET-IT®
BEST OF
Fall Recipes

QUICK AND DELICIOUS
SLOW COOKER MEALS

HOPE COMERFORD

Good Books
New York, New York

Good Books books may be purchased in bulk at special discounts for sales promotion, corporate gifts, fund-raising, or educational purposes. Special editions can also be created to specifications. For details, contact the Special Sales Department, Good Books, 307 West 36th Street, 11th Floor, New York, NY 10018 or info@skyhorsepublishing.com.

Good Books is an imprint of Skyhorse Publishing, Inc.®, a Delaware corporation.

Visit our website at www.goodbooks.com.

10 9 8 7 6 5 4 3 2 1

Library of Congress Cataloging-in-Publication Data is available on file.

Cover design by Mona Lin
Cover photo credit: Meredith Special Interest Media
Interior photo credit: Meredith Special Interest Media

Print ISBN: 978-1-68099-535-0
Ebook ISBN: 978-1-68099-546-6

Printed in China

Table of Contents

Welcome to Fix-It and Forget-It Best of Fall Recipes

As the colors start to change outside and the air grows a bit cooler, the cravings for those fall flavors we all love so much begin to creep in. Enter *Fix-It and Forget-It Best of Fall Recipes*! You'll find lots of warm goodness for your slow cooker in this book, including those delicious autumn flavors like pumpkin, cinnamon, and apple! So, grab a hot cup of cider and cozy up with a blanket as you flip through all of the fall deliciousness this book is about to bring you!

Choosing a Slow Cooker
Not all slow cookers are created equal . . . or work equally as well for everyone!

Those of us who use slow cookers frequently know we have our own preferences when it comes to which slow cooker we choose to use. For instance, I love my programmable slow cooker, but there are many programmable slow cookers I've tried that I've strongly disliked. Why? Because some go by increments of 15 or 30 minutes and some go by 4, 6, 8, or 10 hours. I dislike those restrictions, but I have family and friends who don't mind them at all! I am also pretty brand loyal when it comes to my manual slow cookers because I've had great success with those and have had unsuccessful moments with slow cookers of other brands. So, which slow cooker(s) is/are best for your household?

It really depends on how many people you're feeding and if you're gone for long periods of time. Here are my recommendations:

For 2–3 person household	3–5 quart slow cooker
For 4–5 person household	5–6 quart slow cooker
For a 6+ person household	6½–7 quart slow cooker

Large slow cooker advantages/disadvantages:

Advantages:
- You can fit a loaf pan or a baking dish into a 6- or 7-quart, depending on the shape of your cooker. That allows you to make bread or cakes, or even smaller quantities of main dishes. (Take your favorite baking dish and loaf pan along when you shop for a cooker to make sure they'll fit inside.)
- You can feed large groups of people, or make larger quantities of food, allowing for leftovers, or meals, to freeze.

Disadvantages:
- They take up more storage room.
- They don't fit as neatly into a dishwasher.
- If your crock isn't ⅔ to ¾ full, you may burn your food.

Small slow cooker advantages/disadvantages:

Advantages:
- They're great for lots of appetizers, for serving hot drinks, for baking cakes straight in the crock, and for dorm rooms or apartments.
- Great option for making recipes of smaller quantities.

Disadvantages:
- Food in smaller quantities tends to cook more quickly than larger amounts. So keep an eye on it.
- Chances are, you won't have many leftovers. So, if you like to have leftovers, a smaller slow cooker may not be a good option for you.

My recommendation:

Have at least two slow cookers; one around 3 to 4 quarts and one 6 quarts or larger. A third would be a huge bonus (and a great advantage to your cooking repertoire!). The advantage of having at least a couple is you can make a larger variety of recipes. Also, you can make at least two or three dishes at once for a whole meal.

Manual vs. Programmable

If you are gone for only 6 to 8 hours a day, a manual slow cooker might be just fine for you. If you are gone for more than eight hours during the day, I would highly recommend purchasing a programmable slow cooker that will switch to warm when the cook time you set is up. It will allow you to cook a wider variety of recipes.

The two I use most frequently are my 4-quart manual slow cooker and my 6½-quart programmable slow cooker. I like that I can make smaller portions in my 4-quart slow cooker on days I don't need or want leftovers, but I also love how my 6½-quart slow cooker can accommodate whole chickens, turkey breasts, hams, or big batches of soups. I use them both often.

Get to know your slow cooker . . .

Plan a little time to get acquainted with your slow cooker. Each slow cooker has its own personality—just like your oven (and your car). Plus, many new slow cookers cook hotter and faster than earlier models. I think that with all of the concern for food safety, the slow cooker manufacturers have amped up their settings so that "High," "Low," and "Warm" are all higher temperatures than in the older models. That means they cook hotter—and therefore, faster—than the first slow cookers. The beauty of these little machines is that they're supposed to cook low and slow. We count on that when we flip the switch in the morning before we leave the house for ten hours or so. So, because none of us knows what kind of temperament our slow cooker has until we try it out, nor how hot it cooks—don't assume anything. Save yourself a disappointment and make the first recipe in your new slow cooker on a day when you're at home. Cook it for the shortest amount of time the recipe calls for. Then, check the food to see if it's done. Or if you start smelling food that seems to be finished, turn off the cooker and rescue your food.

Also, all slow cookers seem to have a "hot spot," which is of great importance to know, especially when baking with your slow cooker. This spot may tend to burn food in that area if you're not careful. If you're baking directly in your slow cooker, I recommend covering the "hot spot" with some foil.

Take notes . . .

Don't be afraid to make notes in your cookbook. It's yours! Chances are, it will eventually get passed down to someone in your family and they will love and appreciate all of your musings. Take note of which slow cooker you used and exactly how long it took to cook the recipe. The next time you make it, you won't need to try to remember. Apply what you learned to the next recipes you make in your cooker. If another recipe says it needs to cook 7 to 9 hours, and you've discovered your slow cooker cooks on the faster side, cook that recipe for 6 to 6½ hours and then check it. You can always cook a recipe longer—but you can't reverse things if it's overdone.

Get creative . . .

If you know your morning is going to be hectic, prepare everything the night before, take it out so the crock warms up to room temperature when you first get up in the morning, then plug it in and turn it on as you're leaving the house.

If you want to make something that has a short cook time and you're going to be gone longer than that, cook it the night before and refrigerate it for the next day. Warm it up when you get home. Or, cook those recipes on the weekend when you know you'll be home and eat them later in the week.

Slow Cooking Tips and Tricks and Other Things You May Not Know

- Slow cookers tend to work best when they're ⅔ to ¾ of the way full. You may need to increase the cooking time if you've exceeded that amount, or reduce it if you've put in less than that. If you're going to exceed that limit, it would be best to reduce the recipe, or split it between two slow cookers. (Remember how I suggested owning at least two or three slow cookers?)

- Keep your veggies on the bottom. That puts them in more direct contact with the heat. The fuller your slow cooker, the longer it will take its contents to cook. Also, the more densely packed the cooker's contents are, the longer they will take to cook. And finally, the larger the chunks of meat or vegetables, the more time they will need to cook.

- Keep the lid on! Every time you take a peek, you lose 20 minutes of cooking time. Please take this into consideration each time you lift the lid! I know, some of you can't help yourself and are going to lift anyway. Just don't forget to tack on 20 minutes to your cook time for each time you peeked!

- Sometimes it's beneficial to remove the lid. If you'd like your dish to thicken a bit, take the lid off during the last half hour to hour of cooking time.

- If you have a big slow cooker (7- to 8-quart), you can cook a small batch in it by putting the recipe ingredients into an oven-safe baking dish or baking pan and then placing that into the cooker's crock. First, put a trivet or some metal jar rings on the bottom of the crock, and then set your dish or pan on top of them. Or a loaf pan may "hook onto" the top ridges of the crock belonging to a large oval cooker and hang there straight and securely, "baking" a cake or quick bread. Cover the cooker and flip it on.

- The outside of your slow cooker will be hot! Please remember to keep it out of reach of children and keep that in mind for yourself as well!

- Get yourself a quick-read meat thermometer and use it! This helps remove the question of whether or not your meat is fully cooked, and helps prevent you from overcooking your meat as well.

Internal Cooking Temperatures:
  - Beef—125–130°F (rare); 140–145°F (medium); 160°F (well-done)
  - Pork—140–145°F (rare); 145–150°F (medium); 160°F (well-done)
  - Turkey and Chicken—165°F
  - Frozen meat: The basic rule of thumb is, don't put frozen meat into the slow cooker. The meat does not reach the proper internal temperature in time. This especially applies to thick cuts of meat! Proceed with caution!

- Add fresh herbs 10 minutes before the end of the cooking time to maximize their flavor.
- If your recipe calls for cooked pasta, add it 10 minutes before the end of the cooking time if the cooker is on High; 30 minutes before the end of the cooking time if it's on Low. Then the pasta won't get mushy.
- If your recipe calls for sour cream or cream, stir it in 5 minutes before the end of the cooking time. You want it to heat but not boil or simmer.

Approximate Slow Cooker Temperatures (Remember, each slow cooker is different):
  - High—212–300°F
  - Low—170–200°F
  - Simmer—185°F
  - Warm—165°F

Cooked and dried bean measurements:
  - 16-ounce can, drained = about 1¾ cups beans
  - 19-ounce can, drained = about 2 cups beans
  - 1 pound of dried beans (about 2½ cups) = 5 cups cooked beans

Appetizers and Dips

Red Pepper Cheese Dip

Makes 4–5 cups

Ideal slow cooker: 3-qt.

2 Tbsp. olive oil

4–6 large red bell peppers, cut into 1-inch squares

Crackers and/or pita bread

8 oz. feta cheese, crumbled

1. Pour oil into slow cooker. Stir in peppers.

2. Cover. Cook on low 2 hours.

3. Serve on crackers or pita bread, topped with feta cheese.

Hot Artichoke Dip

Makes 28 servings (7–8 cups)

Ideal slow cooker: 3-qt.

2 (14¾-oz.) jars marinated
artichoke hearts, drained

1½ cups mayonnaise

1½ cups sour cream

1 cup water chestnuts, chopped

¼ cup grated Parmesan cheese

¼ cup finely chopped green onions

1. Cut artichoke hearts into small pieces. Place in a large bowl. Add remaining ingredients and stir well. Pour into slow cooker.

2. Cover and cook on high 1 to 2 hours or on low 3 to 4 hours.

3. Serve with crackers or crusty French bread.

Curried Almonds

Makes 4 cups

Ideal slow cooker: 3-qt.

2 Tbsp. butter, melted

1 Tbsp. curry powder

1 tsp. seasoned salt

1 lb. blanched almonds

1. Combine butter, curry powder, and seasoned salt in a small bowl.

2. Place almonds in slow cooker.

3. Pour butter mixture over almonds, stirring to coat.

4. Cover and cook on low 2 to 3 hours. Increase heat to high. Uncover slow cooker and cook 1 to 1½ hours more.

Baked Brie with Cranberry Chutney

Makes 8–10 servings

Ideal slow cooker: 1- or 1½-qt.

1 cup fresh cranberries
½ cup packed brown sugar
⅓ cup cider vinegar
2 Tbsp. water or orange juice
2 tsp. minced crystallized ginger
¼ tsp. cinnamon
⅛ tsp. ground cloves
Vegetable oil
1 (8-oz.) round Brie cheese
Garnish: fresh mint leaves

1. Combine first 7 ingredients in slow cooker.

2. Cover and cook on low 4 hours. If mixture has not thickened near the end, remove lid, increase heat to high, and cook, uncovered, 30 minutes more.

3. Place cranberry chutney in a covered container and chill for up to 2 weeks. When ready to serve, bring to room temperature.

4. Brush an ovenproof plate with vegetable oil, place unpeeled Brie on plate, and bake, uncovered, at 350°F for 9 minutes or until cheese is soft. Top with chutney. Garnish, if desired. Serve with crackers.

Hearty Pizza Dip

Makes 18 servings

Ideal slow cooker: 3-qt.

1 lb. bulk smoked sausage

2 (8-oz.) pkg. cream cheese, cubed

2 cups pizza sauce

2 cups shredded mozzarella cheese

1 cup shredded cheddar cheese

1. Brown sausage in a skillet, breaking it into small pieces with a spoon as it browns. Drain.

2. Place sausage in slow cooker. Stir in remaining ingredients.

3. Cover and cook on high 1 hour. Stir.

4. Cover and cook on low 2 hours more or until heated through.

5. Serve with corn chips.

Variation:

For a stick-to-the-ribs breakfast, stir 2 tablespoons of the finished dip into 3 eggs while scrambling them. Serve the mixture open-faced on toasted English muffins.

Hot Cheese-and-Bacon Dip

Makes 6–8 servings

Ideal slow cooker: 1- or 1½-qt.

16 slices bacon, diced

2 (8-oz.) pkg. cream cheese, cubed and softened

4 cups shredded mild cheddar cheese

1 cup half-and-half

2 tsp. Worcestershire sauce

1 tsp. dried minced onion

½ tsp. dry mustard

½ tsp. salt

2–3 drops hot sauce

1. Brown and drain bacon. Set aside.

2. Mix remaining ingredients in slow cooker.

3. Cover and cook on low 1 hour, stirring occasionally, until cheese melts. Stir in bacon.

Serving suggestion:

Serve with fruit slices or French bread slices. (Dip fruit in lemon juice to prevent browning.)

Hot Crab Dip

Makes 15–20 servings

Ideal slow cooker: 2½-qt.

½ cup milk

⅓ cup salsa

3 (8-oz.) pkg. cream cheese, cubed

2 (8-oz.) pkg. imitation crabmeat, flaked

I cup thinly sliced green onions

I (4-oz.) can chopped green chilies

Chopped green onions (optional)

1. Combine milk and salsa in a bowl. Transfer to greased slow cooker.

2. Stir in cream cheese, crabmeat, onions, and chilies.

3. Cover and cook on low 2 to 3 hours or until hot and blended, stirring every 30 minutes. Garnish with chopped green onions, if desired.

4. Serve with crackers or bread.

Shortcut Fondue Dip

Makes 8–10 servings

Ideal slow cooker: 1½- or 2-qt.

2 (10¾-oz.) cans condensed cheese soup

2 cups shredded sharp cheddar cheese

1 Tbsp. Worcestershire sauce

1 tsp. lemon juice

2 Tbsp. dried chopped chives

1. Combine soup, cheese, Worcestershire sauce, lemon juice, and chives in slow cooker.

2. Cover and cook on low 2 to 2½ hours. Stir until smooth and well blended.

Serving suggestion:

Serve warm dip with celery sticks, cauliflower florets, and corn chips.

Hot Cheddar-Mushroom Spread

Makes 3¼–3½ cups

Ideal slow cooker: 2-qt.

1 cup mayonnaise

1 cup shredded cheddar cheese

⅓ cup grated Parmesan cheese

2 (4-oz.) cans sliced
mushrooms, drained

½ (1-oz.) envelope ranch
salad dressing mix

Chopped fresh parsley

1. Combine mayonnaise, cheeses, mushrooms, and dressing mix in slow cooker.

2. Cover and cook on low 1 hour or until cheeses are melted and dip is heated through.

3. Sprinkle with parsley before serving.

Serving suggestion:
Serve with toasted bread slices.

Snappy Meatballs

Makes 25 appetizer servings

Ideal slow cooker: 5- to 6-qt.

Meatballs:

2 lb. ground beef

½ cup chopped onion

1 cup bread crumbs

2 eggs

1 tsp. salt

Sauce:

3½ cups tomato juice

1 cup brown sugar

¼ cup white vinegar

1 tsp. grated onion

12 gingersnap cookies, crushed

1. Combine meatball ingredients in a large bowl. Shape into balls. Brown in skillet. Drain well. Spoon into slow cooker.

2. Combine sauce ingredients in a bowl. Pour over meatballs. Mix gently.

3. Cover and cook on low 4 hours.

Salmon-Stuffed Mushrooms

Makes 20 mushrooms

Ideal slow cooker: 6-qt.

20 large fresh button mushrooms

I Tbsp. extra-virgin olive oil
or hazelnut oil

¼ cup chopped red onions

2 Tbsp. chopped hazelnuts, walnuts,
or pecans

½ tsp. Worcestershire sauce

¼ tsp. chopped fresh dill

¼ tsp. salt

4 oz. smoked or steamed
salmon, flaked

Salmon roe (optional)

Chopped fresh dill (optional)

1. Clean mushrooms and remove stems. Place mushrooms, stem-side up, in the bottom of slow cooker.

2. Cover and cook on low 2 hours or until mushrooms are just tender.

3. While mushrooms cook, combine oil and onions in a microwave-safe bowl. Cover. Microwave on high 1 to 1½ minutes or until onions are slightly soft.

4. Add nuts, Worcestershire sauce, dill, and salt to onion mixture. Stir in salmon. Let stand 20 minutes.

5. Remove mushrooms from slow cooker. Turn mushroom caps upside down on paper towels to drain.

6. When cool enough to handle, fill caps with salmon mixture and return to slow cooker, filled side up.

7. Cover and cook on high 10 to 15 minutes or until salmon mixture is bubbly. If desired, sprinkle with salmon roe and chopped dill just before serving.

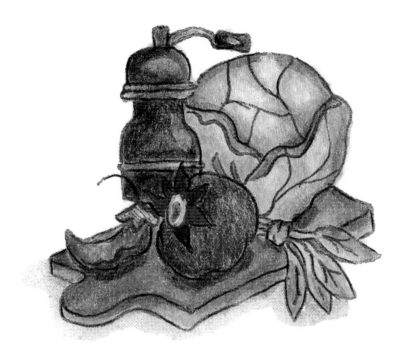

soups and stews

Minestra Di Ceci

Makes 4–6 servings
Ideal slow cooker: 4-qt.

1 lb. dry chickpeas

1 sprig fresh rosemary

10 leaves fresh sage

2 Tbsp. salt

1–2 large garlic cloves, minced

Olive oil

1 cup uncooked small pasta, your choice of shape, or uncooked penne

Garnish: rosemary sprigs

1. Place washed chickpeas in slow cooker. Cover with water. Stir in rosemary, sage, and salt. Soak 8 hours, or overnight.

2. Drain water and remove herbs. Refill slow cooker with peas and fresh water to 1 inch above peas. Cover and cook on low for 5 hours.

3. After 5 hours, puree half of peas, along with several cups of broth from cooker, in blender. Return puree to slow cooker.

4. Sauté garlic in olive oil in skillet. Add to slow cooker.

5. Boil pasta in saucepan until al dente, about 5 minutes. Drain. Add to beans. Cover and cook on high 30 to 60 minutes, or until pasta is tender. Garnish with rosemary sprigs.

Chicken and Rice Soup

Makes 8 servings

Ideal slow cooker: 3½-qt.

½ cup uncooked wild rice

½ cup uncooked long-grain rice

1 tsp. vegetable oil

1 lb. boneless, skinless chicken breast halves, cut into ¾-inch cubes

5¼ cups chicken broth

2 celery ribs, cut into ½-inch pieces (1 cup)

1 medium onion, chopped

2 tsp. dried thyme

¼ tsp. dried crushed red pepper

1. Mix wild and white rice with oil in slow cooker.

2. Cover and cook on high 15 minutes.

3. Add chicken, broth, vegetables, and seasonings.

4. Cover and cook on high 4 to 5 hours or on low 7 to 8 hours.

Serving suggestion:
Garnish each serving with sour cream sprinkled with finely chopped green onions.

Judy's Beef Stew

Makes 4–6 servings

Ideal slow cooker: 5-qt.

2 lb. beef stew meat

5 carrots, sliced

1 onion, diced

3 celery ribs, diced

5 potatoes, cubed

1 (28-oz.) can stewed tomatoes

⅓–½ cup dry quick-cooking tapioca

2 tsp. salt

½ tsp. pepper

1. Combine all ingredients in slow cooker.

2. Cover and cook on high 5 to 6 hours or on low 10 to 12 hours.

Variation:

Add 1 whole clove and 2 bay leaves to stew before cooking. Add 1 cup frozen peas 1 hour before end of cooking time.

Norma's Vegetarian Chili

Makes 8–10 servings

idea slow cooker: 5-qt.

2 Tbsp. oil

2 cups minced celery

1½ cups chopped green bell pepper

1 cup minced onions

4 garlic cloves, minced

5½ cups stewed tomatoes

2 (1-lb.) cans kidney beans, undrained

1½–2 cups raisins

¼ cup wine vinegar

1 Tbsp. chopped parsley

2 tsp. salt

1½ tsp. dried oregano

1½ tsp. cumin

¼ tsp. pepper

¼ tsp. Tabasco sauce

1 bay leaf

¾ cup cashews

1 cup grated cheddar cheese (optional)

1. Combine all ingredients except cashews and cheese in slow cooker.

2. Cover. Simmer on low 8 hours. Add cashews and simmer 30 minutes more.

3. Top individual servings with cheese.

15-Bean Soup

Makes 12 servings

Ideal slow cooker: 6-qt.

1 (20-oz.) pkg. dried 15-bean soup mix

2 cups chopped carrots

1½ cups chopped celery

1 cup chopped onions

2 Tbsp. tomato paste

1 tsp. dried basil

½ tsp. dried oregano

¼ tsp. pepper

5 (14½-oz.) cans chicken or vegetable broth (about 9 cups)

1 (14½-oz.) can diced tomatoes

¼ cup chopped fresh parsley (optional)

1. Combine all ingredients except tomatoes and parsley in slow cooker.

2. Cover and cook on low 10 hours or until beans are tender.

3. Stir in tomatoes, and parsley, if desired.

4. Cover and cook on high 10 to 20 minutes or until soup is thoroughly heated.

TIP

You can use 2¼ cups dried beans of your choice instead of the bean soup mix.

Onion Soup

3 cups thinly sliced onions

¼ cup butter

3 Tbsp. sugar

2 Tbsp. flour

4 cups beef broth

1. Cook onions in butter in large nonstick skillet or saucepan. Cover and cook 15 minutes, stirring frequently. Then add sugar and flour, mixing well. While onions are cooking, place broth in slow cooker on high. Add onion mixture to broth.

2. Cover and cook on low 6 to 8 hours.

Serving suggestion:

Serve topped with toasted bread and grated Parmesan cheese, if desired.

Butternut Squash and Apple Soup

Makes 12 servings

Ideal slow cooker: 8-qt.

2 Tbsp. unsalted butter

2 Tbsp. olive oil

4 cups chopped yellow onion

2 Tbsp. mild curry powder

5 lb. butternut squash (2 large squash)

1½ lb. sweet apples

2 tsp. salt

½ tsp. freshly ground pepper

2 cups water

2 cups apple cider or juice

Garnish: freshly ground pepper

1. Cook butter, olive oil, onion, and curry powder in a large stockpot over low heat until onion is tender, 15 to 20 minutes.

2. Peel squash and remove seeds. Cut squash into chunks.

3. Peel, core, and cut apples into 8 wedges each.

4. Add squash, apples, salt, pepper, and water to pot. Cook until soft enough to puree.

5. Process in a food processor or blender until smooth.

6. Pour entire mixture into slow cooker. Add apple cider or juice.

7. Cover and cook on low 1 to 2 hours. Serve hot from slow cooker. Garnish, if desired.

Harry's Vegetable Soup

Makes 16 servings

Ideal slow cooker: 4-qt.

4 (15¼-oz.) cans mixed vegetables, drained

1 (46-oz.) can vegetable juice

4 cups beef broth

1 tsp. of your favorite seasoning blend (like Mrs. Dash)

1. Mix all ingredients in a greased slow cooker.

2. Cover and cook on low 4 hours or on high 2 hours.

TIP

If you have a beef roast, you may want to add a pound of cut-up pieces in Step 1. Leftover vegetables may be used instead of canned vegetables.

Everyone's Hungry Soup

Makes 20–25 servings

Ideal slow cooker: Two 6- or 7-qt. cookers

6 thick slices bacon

3 lb. boneless beef stewing meat, cubed

1 lb. boneless pork, cubed

3 (14½-oz.) cans stewed, or diced, tomatoes

1 (10-oz.) can tomatoes with chilies

3 celery ribs, chopped

3 large onions, chopped

Garlic to taste

Salt to taste

Pepper to taste

½ cup Worcestershire sauce

2 Tbsp. chili powder

2 cups water

6–8 medium potatoes, peeled and cubed

1 lb. carrots, sliced

1 (15-oz.) can peas, undrained

1 (14½-oz.) can green beans, undrained

1 lb. cut-up okra (optional)

1. Fry bacon in skillet until crisp. Remove bacon, but reserve drippings. Crumble bacon and divide between two large (6-qt. or larger) slow cookers.

2. Brown stewing beef and pork in skillet in bacon drippings. Drain off drippings.

3. Divide beef and pork between two cookers.

4. In a large bowl, combine all remaining ingredients and mix well. Divide between slow cookers.

5. Stir each cooker's ingredients well. Cover. Cook on low 8 to 10 hours.

Serving suggestion:
Serve with loaves of homemade bread or pans of corn bread.

Curried Chicken Chowder

Makes 6–8 servings

Ideal slow cooker: 4-qt.

2 chicken leg quarters, skinned

I onion, chopped

I cup chopped celery, leaves included

I medium potato, diced

3 carrots, sliced

I cup frozen green beans

I ½ tsp. salt

I Tbsp. curry powder, *divided*

I bay leaf

5 cups water

I apple, peeled and diced

3 Tbsp. all-purpose flour

⅓ cup half-and-half, at room temperature

Garnish: chopped fresh parsley

1. Place chicken in slow cooker. Add chopped onion, celery, potato, carrots, green beans, salt, 1½ teaspoons curry powder, and bay leaf. Pour 5 cups water over vegetables.

2. Cover and cook on low 6 to 8 hours.

3. Remove chicken. Add diced apple and remaining 1½ teaspoons curry powder.

4. Remove chicken from bones and return meat to slow cooker.

5. Whisk together flour and half-and-half in a small bowl until completely smooth. Whisk into hot soup. Cover and cook on low 25 to 30 minutes more, stirring once or twice, until mixture is thick and apple is softened. Remove bay leaf before serving. Garnish, if desired.

Hearty Beef-Barley Soup

Makes 8 servings

Ideal slow cooker: 5-qt.

2 lb. beef chuck roast

3 cups tomato juice

1 cup red wine

4 cups water

3 Tbsp. soy sauce

1 bay leaf

½–1 tsp. salt

¼ tsp. freshly ground black pepper

1 onion, diced

2 celery ribs, finely chopped

2 carrots, diced or shredded

1 cup uncooked quick-cooking barley

¼ tsp. dried thyme

1. Place first 11 ingredients in slow cooker.

2. Cover and cook on low 8 hours.

3. Remove roast and shred or chop meat. Return meat to slow cooker.

4. Add barley and thyme. Cover and cook 30 to 60 minutes more or until barley is tender.

Mexican Chicken Tortilla Soup

Makes 6–8 servings

Ideal slow cooker: 6-qt.

6 bone-in chicken thighs, skin removed

2 (15-oz.) cans black beans, undrained

2 (15-oz.) cans Mexican stewed tomatoes or diced tomatoes and green chilies

1 cup salsa—mild, medium, or hot, according to your taste preference

1 (4-oz.) can chopped green chilies

1 (14½-oz.) can tomato sauce

Tortilla chips

2 cups shredded cheddar cheese

1. Combine all ingredients except chips and cheese in slow cooker. Cover and cook on low 6 to 8 hours or until meat is tender.

2. Remove chicken from soup. Remove chicken from bones and cut into bite-size pieces. Stir chicken into soup.

3. To serve, place chips in each individual soup bowl. Ladle soup over chips and top with cheese.

Chinese Chicken Soup

Makes 6 servings

Ideal slow cooker: 4-qt.

3 (14½-oz.) cans chicken broth

1 (16-oz.) pkg. frozen stir-fry vegetable blend

2 cups cubed cooked chicken

1 tsp. minced fresh ginger

1 tsp. soy sauce

1. Combine all ingredients in slow cooker.

2. Cover and cook on high 1 to 2 hours, depending upon how crunchy or soft you like your vegetables.

Chicken-Rice Soup

Makes 8 servings

Ideal slow cooker: 4- or 6-qt.

4 cups chicken broth

4 cups chopped cooked chicken

1⅓ cups chopped celery

1⅓ cups diced carrots

4 cups water

1 cup uncooked long grain rice

1. Combine all ingredients in slow cooker.

2. Cover and cook on low 4 to 8 hours or until vegetables are cooked to your liking.

Chicken Stew with Peppers and Pineapples

Makes 4 servings

Ideal slow cooker: 4-qt.

I lb. boneless, skinless chicken breast halves, cut in 1½-inch cubes

4 medium carrots, sliced into 1-inch pieces

½ cup chicken broth

2 Tbsp. ginger, chopped

1 Tbsp. brown sugar

2 Tbsp. soy sauce

½ tsp. ground allspice

½ tsp. hot pepper sauce

1 (8-oz.) can pineapple chunks, drained, with juice reserved

1 Tbsp. cornstarch

1 medium sweet green pepper, cut in 1-inch pieces

1. Combine chicken, carrots, chicken broth, ginger, sugar, soy sauce, allspice, and hot pepper sauce in slow cooker.

2. Cover. Cook on low 5 to 6 hours or on high 2½ to 3 hours, or until chicken is tender.

3. Combine pineapple juice and cornstarch in bowl until smooth. Stir into chicken mixture.

4. Add pineapple chunks and bell pepper.

5. Cover. Cook on high 15 minutes, or until sauce is slightly thickened.

Serving suggestion:
Serve over cooked rice.

Variation:
Add 1 cut-up fresh tomato 30 minutes before end of cooking time.

Corn and Shrimp Chowder

Makes 6 servings

Ideal slow cooker: 3½-qt.

4 slices bacon, diced

1 cup chopped onions

2 cups diced, unpeeled red potatoes or frozen hash browns

2 (10-oz.) pkg. frozen corn

1 tsp. Worcestershire sauce

½ tsp. paprika

½ tsp. salt

⅛ tsp. pepper

2 cups water

2 (6-oz.) cans shrimp or ¾ lb. cooked and peeled shrimp

1 (12-oz.) can evaporated milk

Chopped fresh chives (optional)

1. Cook bacon in a skillet until crisp. Remove and drain bacon, reserving drippings.

2. Add onions to drippings and sauté just until softened. Transfer onions to slow cooker using a slotted spoon.

3. Add potatoes and next 6 ingredients to cooker.

4. Cover and cook on low 2½ to 3½ hours.

5. Stir in shrimp and evaporated milk. Cover and cook on low 30 minutes more.

6. Just before serving, stir in chives, if desired.

Pork-Sweet Potato Stew

Makes 4 servings

Ideal slow cooker: 3-qt.

1 lb. ground pork

½ cup chopped onion

1 sweet potato, peeled and cubed (about 3 cups)

2 beef bouillon cubes

½ tsp. dried rosemary

3 cups water

1. Cook ground pork and onion in a large nonstick skillet, stirring frequently to break up clumps, until pork is no longer pink. Drain.

2. Place pork and onion in slow cooker. Add remaining ingredients.

3. Cover and cook on low 4 hours.

Variation:

Add a bit of hot sauce to make the stew spicy or serve on the side to accommodate those who like milder food.

Easy Southern Brunswick Stew

Makes 10–12 servings

Ideal slow cooker: 4-qt.

2–3 lb. pork butt

1 (17-oz.) can white corn

1 (14-oz.) bottle ketchup

2 cups diced cooked potatoes

1 (10-oz.) pkg. frozen peas

2 (10¾-oz.) cans tomato soup

Hot sauce to taste

Salt to taste

Pepper to taste

1. Place pork in slow cooker.

2. Cover and cook on high 1 hour. Turn temperature to low and continue cooking 5 to 7 hours more. Remove meat from bone and shred.

3. Combine pork and remaining ingredients in slow cooker.

4. Cover. Bring to boil on high. Turn temperature to low and simmer 30 minutes more.

Caribbean-Style Black Bean Soup

Makes 8 servings

Ideal slow cooker: 4-qt.

1 lb. dried black beans, rinsed and stones removed

4 qt. water

3 onions, chopped

1 green bell pepper, chopped

4 garlic cloves, minced

1 lean ham hock or ¾ cup lean cubed ham

1 Tbsp. oil

1 Tbsp. ground cumin

1–2 tsp. dried oregano, according to your taste preference

¼–1 tsp. dried thyme, according to your taste preference

1 tsp. salt

½ tsp. black pepper

3 cups water

2 Tbsp. vinegar

½ cup fat-free sour cream

Fresh cilantro

1. Soak beans overnight in 4 quarts water. Drain.

2. Combine soaked beans, onions, green pepper, garlic, ham hock, oil, cumin, oregano, thyme, salt, black pepper, and 3 cups water in cooker. Stir well.

3. Cover and cook on high 4 to 5 hours or on low 8 to 10 hours.

4. For a thick soup, remove half of cooked bean mixture; puree until smooth in blender or mash with potato masher. Return to cooker. If you like a thinner soup, leave as is.

5. Add vinegar and stir well. If you used a ham hock, debone the ham, cut into bite-size pieces, and return to soup.

6. Serve soup in bowls with a dollop of sour cream in the middle of each individual serving and top with fresh cilantro.

Carl's Steak Chili

Makes 4 servings

Ideal slow cooker: 3-qt.

1 (16-oz.) can kidney beans, drained

1 (14½-oz.) can diced tomatoes

1 lb. lean top round steak, trimmed of fat and cubed

½ medium onion, diced

⅓ green bell pepper, diced

1 garlic clove, minced

½ Tbsp. chili powder

¼ tsp. black pepper

½ tsp. salt

1 (15-oz.) can low-sodium tomato sauce

Several drops of hot sauce (optional)

Garnishes: sour cream and shredded cheddar cheese

1. Combine all ingredients except garnishes in slow cooker. Stir. Cover and cook on low 8 hours. Garnish with sour cream and cheddar cheese, if desired.

Double Cheese Cauliflower Soup

Makes 6 servings

Ideal slow cooker: 3½- or 4-qt.

4 cups cauliflower pieces (1 small head)

2 cups water

1 (8-oz.) pkg. cream cheese, cubed

1 (5-oz.) jar American cheese spread

¼ lb. dried beef, torn into strips or shredded

½ cup potato flakes or buds

1. Combine cauliflower and 2 cups water in a saucepan. Bring to a boil. Set aside.

2. Heat slow cooker on low. Add cream cheese and cheese spread. Pour in cauliflower and water. Stir cheese until dissolved and thoroughly mixed with cauliflower.

3. Add dried beef and potato flakes. Mix well.

4. Cover and cook on low 2 to 3 hours.

Steak Soup

Makes 10–12 servings
Ideal slow cooker: 4- to 5-qt.

2 lb. ground beef

5 cups water

1 large onion, chopped

4 celery ribs, chopped

3 carrots, sliced

2 (14½-oz.) cans diced tomatoes

1 (10-oz.) pkg. frozen mixed vegetables

5 Tbsp. beef-base granules
or 5 beef bouillon cubes

½ tsp. pepper

½ cup butter, melted

½ cup all-purpose flour

2 tsp. salt

1. Combine beef and next 8 ingredients in slow cooker.

2. Cover. Cook on high 4 to 6 hours or on low 8 to 12 hours.

3. One hour before serving, turn to high. Make a paste of melted butter and flour. Stir until smooth. Pour into slow cooker and stir until well blended. Add salt.

4. Cover. Continue cooking on high until thickened.

Crabmeat Soup

Makes 8 servings

Ideal slow cooker: 3½-qt.

2 (10¾-oz.) cans cream
of tomato soup

2 (10½-oz.) cans split pea soup

4 cups milk

I cup heavy cream

I or 2 (6-oz.) cans crabmeat, drained

¼ cup sherry (optional)

1. Pour soups into slow cooker. Add milk and stir to mix. Cover and cook on low 4 hours or until hot.

2. Stir in cream and crabmeat. Continue to cook on low 1 hour more or until heated through.

Buffalo Chicken Wing Soup

Makes 8 servings

Ideal slow cooker: 3-qt.

6 cups milk

3 (10¾-oz.) cans condensed cream of chicken soup

3 cups shredded or cubed cooked chicken (about 1 lb.)

1 cup (8 oz.) sour cream

1–8 Tbsp. hot sauce, according to your taste preference

1. Combine milk and soup in slow cooker until smooth.

2. Stir in chicken.

3. Cover and cook on low 3½ to 4½ hours.

4. Stir in sour cream and hot sauce. Cover and cook 15 minutes more.

TIP

Start with a small amount of hot sauce and then add more to suit your tastes.

Chicken Noodle Soup

Makes 6–8 servings

Ideal slow cooker: 4-qt.

2 (10¾-oz.) cans cream of chicken-mushroom soup

5 cups water

2 cups chopped cooked chicken

1 (10-oz.) pkg. frozen mixed vegetables

½–1 tsp. pepper

1½ cups uncooked egg noodles

1. Place soup in slow cooker. Blend in 5 cups water. Stir in chicken, vegetables, and pepper.

2. Cover and cook on high 3 to 4 hours or on low 6 to 8 hours.

3. Turn to high if using low setting. Stir in noodles.

4. Cover and cook 20 to 30 minutes or until noodles are just tender.

Variation:

Substitute other flavors of cream soups for the chicken-mushroom soup. Use chicken broth in place of all or part of the water.

Lentil-Tomato Stew

Makes 8 servings

Ideal slow cooker: 6-qt.

3 cups water

1 (28-oz.) can low-sodium peeled Italian tomatoes, undrained

1 (6-oz.) can low-sodium tomato paste

½ cup dry red wine

¾ tsp. dried basil

¾ tsp. dried thyme

½ tsp. dried crushed red pepper

1 lb. dried lentils, rinsed and drained with stones removed

1 large onion, chopped

4 medium carrots, cut into ½-inch rounds

4 medium celery ribs, cut into ½-inch slices

3 garlic cloves, minced

1 tsp. salt

Chopped fresh basil or parsley

1. Combine 3 cups water, tomatoes with juice, tomato paste, wine, basil, thyme, and crushed red pepper in slow cooker.

2. Break up tomatoes with a wooden spoon; stir to blend them and the paste into the mixture.

3. Add lentils, onion, carrots, celery, and garlic.

4. Cover and cook on high 4 to 5 hours or on low 10 to 12 hours.

5. Stir in salt.

6. Serve in bowls and sprinkle with chopped basil or parsley.

Nine-Bean Soup with Tomatoes

Makes 8–10 servings

Ideal slow cooker: 6.-qt.

2 cups dry nine-bean soup mix

I lb. ham, diced

I large onion, chopped

I garlic clove, minced

½–¾ tsp. salt

2 qt. water

I (16-oz.) can tomatoes, undrained and chopped

I (10-oz.) can tomatoes with green chilies, undrained

Garnish: fresh cilantro (optional)

1. Sort and wash bean mix. Place in slow cooker. Cover with water 2 inches above beans. Let soak overnight. Drain.

2. Add ham, onion, garlic, salt, and 2 quarts water.

3. Cover and cook on low 7 hours.

4. Add tomatoes and continue cooking on low 1 hour. Stir occasionally. Garnish, if desired.

NOTE

Nine-bean soup mix is a mix of barley pearls, black beans, red beans, pinto beans, navy beans, great northern beans, lentils, split peas, and black-eyed peas.

Veggie Stew

Makes 10–15 servings

Ideal slow cooker: 8-qt.

5–6 potatoes, diced

3 carrots, diced

1 onion, chopped

½ cup chopped celery

2 cups canned diced
or stewed tomatoes

3 vegetable bouillon cubes dissolved in
3 cups water

1½ tsp. dried thyme

½ tsp. dried parsley

½ cup brown rice, uncooked

1 lb. frozen green beans

1 lb. frozen corn

1 (15-oz.) can butter beans

1 (46-oz.) can vegetable juice
(we used V8)

1. Combine potatoes and next 8 ingredients in 8-quart slow cooker or two medium-size slow cookers.

2. Cover and cook on high 2 hours. Puree one cup of mixture, and stir into slow cooker to thicken soup.

3. Stir in beans and remaining ingredients.

4. Cover and cook on high 1 hour and then on low 6 to 8 hours.

Lidia's Egg Drop Soup

Makes 8 servings

Ideal slow cooker: 3½-qt.

2 (14½-oz.) cans fat-free, low-sodium chicken broth

1 qt. water

2 Tbsp. fish sauce

¼ tsp. salt

¼ cup cornstarch

1 cup cold water

2 eggs, beaten

1 green onion, chopped

¼ tsp. pepper

1. Combine broth and water in a large saucepan.

2. Add fish sauce and salt. Bring to a boil.

3. Mix cornstarch into 1 cup cold water in a bowl until smooth. Add to soup. Bring to a boil while stirring. Remove from heat.

4. Pour beaten eggs into thickened broth, but do not stir. Instead, pull a fork through soup with two strokes.

5. Transfer to slow cooker. Add green onion and pepper.

6. Cover and cook on low 1 hour. Keep warm in slow cooker until ready to serve.

7. Serve alone or with rice.

Beef Tortellini Soup

Makes 6 servings

Ideal slow cooker: 4- to 5-qt.

1 lb. ground beef

Oil (optional)

2 (14½-oz.) cans stewed or diced tomatoes

1 (10½-oz.) can condensed French onion soup

1 (9-oz.) pkg. frozen green beans

1 (9-oz.) pkg. refrigerated cheese tortellini

1 medium zucchini, chopped

1 tsp. dried basil

½–¾ tsp. salt

¼ tsp. pepper

3½ cups water

Garnish: chopped fresh parsley

1. Brown beef in oil, if needed, in a skillet over medium heat. Stir frequently to crumble. When beef is no longer pink, drain.

2. Place beef in slow cooker. Stir in remaining ingredients except garnish.

3. Cover and cook on low 8 hours. Sprinkle with parsley.

Beef Stew with Shiitake Mushrooms

Makes 4–6 servings

Ideal slow cooker: 5-qt.

12 new potatoes, quartered

½ cup chopped onion

1 (8-oz.) pkg. baby carrots

1 (3.4-oz.) pkg. fresh shiitake mushrooms, sliced, or 2 cups button mushrooms, sliced

1 (16-oz.) can whole tomatoes

1 (14½-oz.) can beef broth

½ cup all-purpose flour

1 Tbsp. Worcestershire sauce

1 tsp. salt

1 tsp. sugar

1 tsp. dried marjoram leaves

¼ tsp. pepper

1 lb. beef stew meat, cubed

1. Combine all ingredients except stew meat in slow cooker. Add beef.

2. Cover and cook on high 1 hour and then on low 6 to 7 hours. Stir well before serving.

Serving idea:

Accompany this dish with mixed salad greens and French bread.

Black Bean and Ham Soup

Makes 8 servings

Ideal slow cooker: 5- to 6-qt.

2 cups dried black beans, rinsed and stones removed

4–6 cups water

2 small onions, chopped

3 garlic cloves, minced

2 tsp. paprika

1½ tsp. ground cumin

¼ tsp. chili powder

2 bay leaves

1 ham hock

1 green bell pepper, chopped

1. Place beans in a large soup pot. Cover with water. Soak or precook them (covered) 30 minutes. Pour off the water.

2. Transfer beans to slow cooker. Add 4 to 6 cups fresh water to the beans.

3. Add onions, garlic, paprika, cumin, chili powder, and bay leaves, stirring well.

4. Submerge ham hock in the liquid in cooker.

5. Cover and cook on high 5 to 7 hours, or on low 9 to 11 hours or until beans and meat are tender. Thirty minutes before end of cooking time, stir in bell pepper.

6. Remove ham hock using a slotted spoon and cool slightly. Pull ham from bone and cut into small pieces. Add ham to soup. Serve soup as is or over cooked rice.

Meaty Mains

Autumn Harvest Pork Loin

Makes 4–6 servings

Ideal slow cooker: 5-qt.

1 cup cider or apple juice

1½–2 lb. pork loin

Salt to taste

Pepper to taste

2 large Granny Smith apples, peeled and sliced

1½ whole butternut squash, peeled and cubed

½ cup brown sugar

¼ tsp. cinnamon

¼ tsp. dried thyme

¼ tsp. dried sage

1. Heat cider in hot skillet. Sear pork loin on all sides in cider.

2. Sprinkle meat with salt and pepper on all sides. Place in slow cooker, along with pan juices.

3. In a large bowl, combine apples and squash. Sprinkle with sugar, cinnamon, and herbs. Stir. Spoon around pork loin in cooker.

4. Cover. Cook on low 5 to 6 hours.

5. Remove pork from cooker. Let stand 10 to 15 minutes. Slice into ½-inch-thick slices.

6. Serve topped with apples and squash.

Asian Pork Roast

Makes 4–6 servings

Ideal slow cooker: 4-qt.

½ cup ketchup

¼ cup soy sauce

¼ cup honey

1 (2½- to 3-lb) pork loin roast

2–3 garlic cloves, sliced

Freshly ground black pepper to taste

3 sprigs fresh rosemary
or 1 tsp. dried rosemary

Garnish: fresh rosemary

1. Combine first 3 ingredients. Set aside.

2. Cut slits into pork loin. Insert garlic slices into slits. Place pork in slow cooker.

3. Pour soy sauce mixture over pork.

4. Sprinkle pepper over pork. Place rosemary on pork.

5. Cover and cook on low 3 to 4 hours or until meat registers 145°F on an instant-read thermometer when inserted into center of pork.

6. Transfer pork to a platter. Cover with foil to keep warm. Let stand 10 to 15 minutes. Spoon soy sauce mixture over meat. Garnish, if desired.

Slurping Good Sausages

Makes 6–8 servings

Ideal slow cooker: 4-qt.

2 lb. sweet Italian sausage,
cut into 5-inch pieces

1 (24-oz.) jar pasta sauce

1 (6-oz.) can tomato paste

1 large green bell pepper,
chopped or cut into thin strips

1 large onion, thinly sliced

1 cup water

1 Tbsp. grated Parmesan cheese,
plus a little more

2 Tbsp. chopped fresh parsley

Grated Parmesan cheese (optional)

Buns (optional)

Cooked pasta (optional)

1. Place sausage pieces in a large skillet and add water to cover. Simmer 10 minutes. Drain.

2. Add pasta sauce and next 5 ingredients to slow cooker. Stir in sausage pieces.

3. Cover and cook on low 6 hours. Just before serving, stir in parsley.

4. Serve in buns, or cut sausage into bite-size pieces and serve over cooked pasta. Sprinkle with Parmesan cheese, if desired.

Brats and Spuds

Makes 6 servings

Ideal slow cooker: 4-qt.

5–6 bratwurst links, cut into 1-inch pieces

1–2 Tbsp. vegetable oil

5 medium potatoes, cut into quarters

1 (27-oz.) can sauerkraut, rinsed and drained

1 medium-size tart apple, chopped

1 small onion, chopped

⅓–½ cup packed brown sugar

½ tsp. salt

1. Brown bratwurst on all sides in oil in a skillet over medium heat.

2. Combine remaining ingredients in slow cooker.

3. Stir in bratwurst and pan drippings.

4. Cover and cook on low 5 to 6 hours, until potatoes and apple are tender.

Pork Barbecue Sandwiches

Makes 8 servings

Ideal slow cooker: 4-qt.

3–4 lb. boneless pork loin roast

1½ tsp. seasoned salt

1 tsp. garlic powder

Dash of pepper

1 cup barbecue sauce

1 cup cola, regular or diet

1. Cut pork roast in half and place in slow cooker.

2. Sprinkle pork with salt, garlic powder, and pepper.

3. Cover and cook on low 4 hours.

4. Place cooked pork on a large platter. Skim fat from broth remaining in cooker.

5. Shred pork using two forks. Return pork to the broth in cooker.

6. Combine barbecue sauce and cola in a small bowl. Add sauce mixture to cooker, stirring to combine.

7. Cover and cook on high 1 to 2 hours or until mixture is thoroughly heated.

Serving suggestion:

Serve the pork barbecue on buns or hoagie rolls or wrap it up in flour tortillas.

Succulent Steak

Makes 6 servings

Ideal slow cooker: 4-qt.

¼ cup all-purpose flour

½ tsp. salt

¼ tsp. pepper

¼ tsp. paprika

1½ lb. round steak (½- to ¾-inch-thick)

2 onions, sliced

1 (4-oz.) can sliced mushrooms, drained

½ cup fat-free, low-sodium beef broth

2 tsp. Worcestershire sauce

2 Tbsp. all-purpose flour

3 Tbsp. water

1. Mix together ¼ cup flour, salt, pepper, and paprika in a shallow dish.

2. Cut steak into 6 pieces. Dredge steak in seasoned flour until lightly coated.

3. Layer half of onions, half of steak, and half of mushrooms in slow cooker. Repeat.

4. Combine beef broth and Worcestershire sauce in a small bowl. Pour over mixture in slow cooker.

5. Cover and cook on low 8 to 10 hours.

6. Transfer steak to a serving platter and keep warm. Mix together 2 tablespoons flour and water in a small bowl. Stir into cooking liquid in slow cooker and cook on high until thickened, about 10 minutes. Pour over steak and serve. Garnish, if desired.

Apple and Onion Beef Pot Roast

Makes 8–10 servings

Ideal slow cooker: 4-qt.

3 lb. boneless beef roast, cut in half

Vegetable oil

1 cup water

1 tsp. seasoning salt

½ tsp. soy sauce

½ tsp. Worcestershire sauce

¼ tsp. garlic powder

1 large tart apple, quartered

1 large onion, sliced

2 Tbsp. cornstarch

2 Tbsp. water

1. Brown roast on all sides in oil in skillet. Transfer to slow cooker.

2. Add water to skillet. Stir with wooden spoon to loosen browned bits. Pour over roast.

3. Sprinkle with seasoning salt, soy sauce, Worcestershire sauce, and garlic powder.

4. Top with apple and onion.

5. Cover. Cook on low 5 to 6 hours.

6. Remove roast and onion. Let stand 15 minutes. To make gravy, pour juices from roast into saucepan and simmer until reduced to 2 cups.

7. Combine cornstarch and water until smooth in small bowl.

8. Stir into beef broth. Bring to boil. Cook and stir 2 minutes, or until thickened.

9. Slice pot roast and serve with gravy.

Mexican Haystacks

Makes 10–12 servings

Ideal slow cooker: 5-qt.

2 lb. ground beef

1 small onion, chopped

2 (8-oz.) cans tomato sauce

2 (15-oz.) cans chili beans with chili gravy, or red beans

2 (10-oz.) cans mild enchilada sauce or mild salsa

1 tsp. garlic salt

½ tsp. chili powder

Pepper to taste

Baked potatoes or cooked rice

Toppings: raisins, chopped apples, fresh pineapple chunks, shredded lettuce, chopped tomatoes, shredded coconut, shredded Monterey Jack cheese, shredded cheddar cheese, corn chips

1. Brown ground beef in a skillet over medium-high heat, stirring until ground beef crumbles and is no longer pink. Using a slotted spoon, lift beef out of drippings and into slow cooker. Discard drippings.

2. Stir onion, tomato sauce, chili beans, enchilada sauce, garlic salt, chili powder, and pepper into beef in slow cooker.

3. Cover and cook on high 1 hour or on low 2 to 3 hours.

4. Serve over baked potatoes or rice. Serve with desired toppings.

Easy Company Beef

Makes 12 servings

Ideal slow cooker: 4-qt.

3 lb. lean beef stew meat

1 (10¾-oz.) can cream
of mushroom soup

1 (7-oz.) jar sliced
mushrooms, undrained

½ cup red wine

1 (1.9-oz.) envelope dry onion soup
mix

1. Combine all ingredients in slow cooker.

2. Cover and cook on low 10 hours.

3. Serve over cooked noodles, rice, or pasta.

Asian Meatballs

Makes 6 servings

Ideal slow cooker: 3-qt.

1 lb. ground beef

1 egg

5 Tbsp. cornstarch, *divided*

½ tsp. salt

2 Tbsp. minced onions

2 cups pineapple juice

2 Tbsp. soy sauce

½ cup wine vinegar

¾ cup water

½ cup sugar

1 green bell pepper, cut into strips

1 can sliced water chestnuts, drained

1. Combine beef, egg, 1 tablespoon cornstarch, salt, and onions in a bowl.

2. Shape into 1-inch balls. Place on an aluminum foil-lined broiler pan. Broil 5 inches from heat until browned all sides, turning occasionally.

3. Combine remaining cornstarch with pineapple juice in a saucepan. Stir in soy sauce, vinegar, water, and sugar. Bring to a boil. Simmer, stirring until thickened.

4. Combine meatballs and pineapple juice mixture in slow cooker.

5. Cover and cook on low 2 hours.

6. Stir in bell pepper and water chestnuts.

7. Cover and cook on low 1 hour more.

Chicken and Sausage Cacciatore

Makes 4–6 servings

Ideal slow cooker: 5-qt.

1 lb. Italian sausage, cut into ½-inch slices

1 lb. boneless, skinless chicken breast halves, cut into 1-inch pieces

Vegetable oil

1 large green bell pepper, sliced in 1-inch strips

1 cup sliced fresh mushrooms

1 medium onion, sliced in rings

½ tsp. dried oregano

½ tsp. dried basil

1½ cups Italian-style tomato sauce

1. Heat oil in a skillet. Lightly brown sausage and chicken breast pieces in skillet. Drain off drippings.

2. Layer vegetables into slow cooker.

3. Top with meat.

4. Sprinkle with oregano and basil.

5. Top with tomato sauce.

6. Cover. Cook on low 3 to 4 hours.

7. Remove cover during last 30 minutes of cooking time to allow sauce to cook off and thicken.

Serving suggestion:
Serve over cooked spiral pasta.

Chicken in Mushroom Gravy

Makes 6 servings

Ideal slow cooker: 4½-qt.

6 boneless, skinless chicken breast halves

Salt and pepper to taste

¼ cup dry white wine or chicken broth

1 (10¾-oz.) can cream of mushroom soup

1 (4-oz.) can sliced mushrooms, drained

1. Place chicken in slow cooker. Season with salt and pepper.

2. Combine wine and soup in a bowl.

3. Pour over chicken.

4. Top with mushrooms.

5. Cover and cook on low 7 to 9 hours.

Salsa Chicken

Makes 8 servings

Ideal slow cooker: 5-qt.

8 boneless, skinless chicken breast halves

3 cups salsa of your choice

¼ cup brown sugar

1. Place chicken in slow cooker.

2. Pour salsa over chicken. If you need to stack chicken, be sure to spoon salsa over all layers.

3. Sprinkle brown sugar over top or over layers of chicken.

4. Cover and cook on low 6 to 8 hours, until chicken is cooked through but not dry or mushy.

Savory Chicken

Makes 4 servings

Ideal slow cooker: 4- or 5-qt.

2½ lb. chicken pieces, skin removed

1 lb. fresh tomatoes, chopped, or 1 (15-oz.) can stewed tomatoes

1 onion, chopped

2 garlic cloves, minced

½ cup chicken broth

2 Tbsp. white wine

1 bay leaf

1½ tsp. salt

1 tsp. dried thyme

¼ tsp. pepper

2 cups broccoli, cut into bite-size pieces

1. Combine all ingredients except broccoli in slow cooker.

2. Cover and cook on low 8 to 10 hours.

3. Add broccoli 30 minutes before serving.

Chicken Sweet and Sour

Makes 8 servings

Ideal slow cooker: 4- or 5-qt.

4 medium potatoes, sliced

8 boneless, skinless chicken breast halves

2 Tbsp. brown sugar

2 Tbsp. cider vinegar

1 tsp. dried basil
or 1 Tbsp. chopped fresh basil

¼ tsp. nutmeg

1 cup orange juice

Dried parsley to taste

1 (17-oz.) can sliced peaches in water, drained

1. Place potatoes in greased slow cooker. Arrange chicken on top.

2. Combine brown sugar, vinegar, basil, nutmeg, and orange juice in a bowl. Pour over chicken. Sprinkle with parsley.

3. Cover and cook on low 6 hours.

4. Remove chicken and potatoes from sauce and arrange on a warm platter.

5. Increase heat to high. Add peaches. Cover and cook until warm.

Serving suggestion:

Spoon peaches and sauce over chicken and potatoes. Garnish with fresh parsley and orange slices.

Fruited Barbecue Chicken

Makes 4–6 servings

Ideal slow cooker: 4-qt.

1 (29-oz.) can tomato sauce

1 (20-oz.) can unsweetened crushed pineapple, undrained

3 Tbsp. vinegar

2 Tbsp. brown sugar

1 Tbsp. instant minced onion

2 tsp. Worcestershire sauce

1 tsp. paprika

¼ tsp. garlic powder

⅛ tsp. pepper

3 lb. boneless, skinless chicken breast halves, cubed

1 (11-oz.) can mandarin oranges, drained

1 (8-oz.) can pineapple chunks, drained

1 Tbsp. sliced green onions

1. Combine first 9 ingredients in slow cooker.

2. Add chicken pieces.

3. Cover and cook on high 4 hours.

4. Just before serving, stir in oranges and pineapple. Sprinkle with green onions.

Serving suggestion:
Serve over hot rice.

French Chicken

Makes 4–6 servings

Ideal slow cooker: 5-qt.

1 lb. baby carrots

2 medium onions, sliced

2 celery ribs, diced

4 garlic cloves, peeled

3 lb. bone-in chicken thighs, skin removed

½ cup white cooking wine or chicken broth

1½ tsp. salt

1 tsp. dried basil

½ tsp. dried marjoram

½ tsp. pepper

2 Tbsp. chopped fresh parsley

1. Place carrots, onions, celery, and garlic in bottom of slow cooker.

2. Lay chicken thighs on top. Pour wine or broth over chicken.

3. Sprinkle with salt, basil, marjoram, and pepper.

4. Cover and cook on low 4½ to 5½ hours, until a meat thermometer inserted in chicken registers 165°F and carrots are tender.

5. Sprinkle with fresh parsley before serving.

Cajun Sausage and Beans

Makes 4–6 servings

Ideal slow cooker: 4-qt.

1 lb. low-fat smoked sausage, cut into ¼-inch pieces

1 (16-oz.) can no-salt-added red kidney beans

1 (16-oz.) can crushed tomatoes with green chilies

1 cup chopped celery

½ onion, chopped

2 Tbsp. dried Italian seasoning

Hot sauce to taste (we used Tabasco)

1. Combine all ingredients in slow cooker.

2. Cover and cook on low 8 hours.

3. Serve over rice or as a soup.

Cheese Tortellini and Meatballs with Vodka Pasta Sauce

Makes 4–6 servings

Ideal slow cooker: 5-qt.

1 (1½-lb.) bag frozen cheese tortellini

1 (1½-lb.) bag frozen Italian-style meatballs

1 (20-oz.) jar vodka pasta sauce

1 (8-oz.) can tomato sauce

1 cup water

1½ tsp. dried oregano

1½ tsp. dried basil

½ tsp. dried crushed red pepper, or less if desired

2 cups shredded mozzarella cheese

Garnish: fresh basil

1. Combine all ingredients except cheese and garnish in greased slow cooker.

2. Cover and cook on low 6 hours.

3. Top each serving with shredded cheese. Garnish, if desired.

Blue Ribbon Cranberry Chicken

Makes 4–6 servings

Ideal slow cooker: 4- to 5-qt.

2½–3 lb. chicken, cut up

1 (16-oz.) can whole-berry cranberry sauce

1 (8-oz.) bottle Russian salad dressing

1 (1-oz.) envelope dry onion soup mix

1. Rinse chicken and pat dry with paper towels. Place chicken in slow cooker.

2. Combine cranberry sauce, salad dressing, and soup mix. Pour over chicken.

3. Cover with slow cooker lid and chill 1 to 8 hours or overnight.

4. Without removing cover, cook on high 4 hours or on high 1 hour and then on low 5 to 7 hours. Serve chicken and sauce over noodles or rice.

Beef Roast with Mushrooms and Barley

Makes 4–6 servings

Ideal slow cooker: 6-qt.

I cup pearl barley (not quick-cooking)

½ cup diced onion

2 (4-oz.) cans mushrooms, undrained

I tsp. minced garlic

I tsp. dried Italian seasoning

¼ tsp. pepper

2–3 lb. beef chuck roast

I¾ cups beef broth

Garnish: chopped fresh parsley (optional)

1. Place barley, onion, mushrooms with liquid, and garlic in slow cooker.

2. Sprinkle Italian seasoning and pepper evenly over top.

3. Add roast. Pour broth over all.

4. Cover and cook on low 6 to 8 hours or until roast is fork-tender and barley is tender. Garnish, if desired.

Curried Chicken & Fruit

Makes 5 servings

Ideal slow cooker: 5-qt.

2½–3½ lb. bone-in chicken thighs, skin removed

½ tsp. salt

¼ tsp. pepper

1–2 Tbsp. curry powder, depending on how much you like curry

1 garlic clove, crushed or minced

1 Tbsp. butter, melted

½ cup chicken broth or 1 chicken bouillon cube dissolved in ½ cup water

2 Tbsp. finely chopped onion

1 (29-oz.) can sliced peaches, undrained

½ cup pitted prunes

3 Tbsp. cornstarch

3 Tbsp. cold water

Cooked rice

Toppings: peanuts, shredded coconut, and fresh pineapple chunks (optional)

1. Place chicken in slow cooker.

2. Combine salt, pepper, curry powder, garlic, butter, broth, and onion in a bowl.

3. Drain peaches, reserving syrup. Add ½ cup syrup to curry mixture. Pour syrup over chicken.

4. Cover and cook on low 4 to 5 hours. Remove chicken from slow cooker to a serving platter. Tent with foil to keep warm.

5. Increase heat to high. Stir prunes into sauce in slow cooker.

6. In a small bowl, dissolve cornstarch in cold water. Stir into hot broth in slow cooker.

7. Cover and cook on high 10 minutes, stirring once or twice, until thickened. Add peaches. Add cooked chicken. (Remove chicken from bones, if desired.)

8. Serve over cooked rice. Top with peanuts, shredded coconut, and fresh pineapple chunks, if desired.

Spicy Chicken Curry

Makes 10 servings

Ideal slow cooker: 4- to 5-qt.

10 skinless chicken
breast halves, *divided*

1 (16-oz.) jar mild, medium,
or hot salsa

1 medium onion, chopped

2 Tbsp. curry powder

1 cup sour cream

1. Place half the chicken in the slow cooker.

2. Combine salsa, onion, and curry powder in a medium bowl. Pour half the sauce over the chicken in the cooker. Repeat layers.

3. Cover and cook on high 3 hours or on high 1½ hours and then on low 3 hours.

4. Remove chicken to serving platter and cover to keep warm.

5. Add sour cream to slow cooker and stir into salsa mixture until well blended. Serve over chicken.

Gourmet Chicken Breasts

Makes 4–6 servings

Ideal slow cooker: 3- to 4-qt.

6–8 slices dried beef

4–6 boneless, skinless chicken breast halves

2–3 slices bacon, cut in half lengthwise

1 (10¾-oz.) can cream of mushroom soup

1 (8-oz.) container sour cream

½ cup all-purpose flour

1. Line bottom of slow cooker with dried beef.

2. Roll up each chicken breast half and wrap with a half-slice of bacon. Place in slow cooker.

3. Combine remaining ingredients in a bowl. Pour over chicken.

4. Cover and cook on high 1 hour and then on low 4 to 6 hours.

5. Serve with cooked noodles, rice, or mashed potatoes.

Cheryl's Macaroni and Cheese

Makes 6 servings

Ideal slow cooker: 2½-qt.

¾ cup dry elbow macaroni, cooked

3–4 cups (about ¾ lb.) shredded sharp cheddar cheese, *divided*

1 (3-oz.) can evaporated milk

1½ cups milk

2 eggs

1 tsp. salt

¼ tsp. black pepper

Chopped onion to taste

1. Combine all ingredients, except 1 cup cheese, in greased slow cooker. Sprinkle reserved cup of cheese over top.

2. Cover and cook on low 3 to 4 hours.

Variation:

For some extra zest, add ½ teaspoon dry mustard when combining all ingredients. Add thin slices of cheese to top of mixture.

Slow-Cooker Beef with Mushrooms

Makes 6 servings

Ideal slow cooker: 3-qt.

2 medium onions, thinly sliced

½ lb. mushrooms, sliced

2½ lb. beef flank or round steak

Salt and pepper to taste

1 Tbsp. Worcestershire sauce

1 Tbsp. vegetable oil

Paprika to taste

1. Place onions and mushrooms in slow cooker.

2. Score top of meat about ½-inch deep in diamond pattern.

3. Season with salt and pepper. Rub in Worcestershire sauce and oil. Sprinkle top with paprika.

4. Place steak on top of onions and mushrooms.

5. Cover and cook on low 7 to 8 hours.

6. To serve, cut beef across grain in thin slices. Top with mushrooms and onions.

Variation:

Add 1 tablespoon lemon juice to Worcestershire sauce and oil in Step 3.

Country Pork and Squash

Makes 6 servings

Ideal slow cooker: 5-qt.

6 boneless country-style pork ribs, trimmed of fat

2 Tbsp. vegetable oil

2 medium acorn squash

¾ cup brown sugar

2 Tbsp. orange juice

¾ tsp. browning and seasoning sauce (we used Kitchen Bouquet)

1. Cook ribs in hot oil in a large skillet over medium-high heat until browned on all sides. Place ribs in slow cooker.

2. Cut each squash in half. Remove seeds. Cut each squash half into 3 slices.

3. Place squash slices on top of ribs.

4. Combine remaining ingredients in a small bowl. Pour sugar mixture over ribs and squash.

5. Cover and cook on low 6 to 8 hours.

Round Steak Casserole

Makes 6 servings

Ideal slow cooker: 4½- to 5-qt.

2 lb. round steak,
cut into ½-inch slices

1 tsp. salt

¼ tsp. pepper

1 onion, thinly sliced

3–4 potatoes, peeled and quartered

1 (16-oz.) can French-style green beans, drained

1 garlic clove, minced

1 (10¾-oz.) can tomato soup

1 (14½-oz.) can tomatoes

1. Season steak with salt and pepper. Cut into serving-size pieces and place in slow cooker.

2. Add onion, potatoes, green beans, and garlic. Top with soup and tomatoes.

3. Cover and cook on high 4 to 5 hours or on low 8 to 10 hours. Remove cover during last half hour if too much liquid has accumulated.

Sweet and Saucy Ribs

Makes 4 servings

Ideal slow cooker: 3- or 4-qt.

2 lb. baby back pork ribs

1 tsp. black pepper

2 Tbsp. vegetable oil

2½ cups barbecue sauce

1 (8-oz.) jar cherry jam or preserves

1 Tbsp. Dijon mustard

¼ tsp. salt

1. Rub ribs with pepper. Cut into 2-rib portions and cook in hot oil in a large skillet over medium-high heat until browned on all sides. Place ribs in slow cooker.

2. Combine remaining ingredients. Pour over ribs, coating each piece.

3. Cover and cook on low 6 to 8 hours.

TIP

Try this delicious recipe using apricot, plum, or grape jam or preserves.

Chicken on a Whim

Makes 6–8 servings

Ideal slow cooker: 5-qt.

6 medium-sized boneless, skinless chicken breast halves

1 small onion, sliced

1 cup dry white wine, chicken broth, or water

1 (4½-oz.) can chicken broth

2 cups water

1 (4½-oz.) can sliced black olives, undrained

1 (17½-oz.) jar marinated artichoke hearts with juice

5 garlic cloves, minced

1 cup uncooked elbow macaroni or small shells

1 envelope dry savory garlic soup

1. Place chicken in slow cooker. Spread onion over chicken.

2. Combine remaining ingredients, except dry soup mix, and pour over chicken. Sprinkle with dry soup.

3. Cover and cook on low 4½ hours, or until chicken is no longer pink in the center.

Serving suggestion:

Serve this dish with mixed salad greens and crusty French bread for a complete one-dish meal.

Chicken and Dumplings

Makes 5–6 servings

Ideal slow cooker: 3- to 4-qt.

I lb. boneless, skinless chicken breast halves, cut into 1-inch cubes

I lb. frozen vegetables of your choice

I medium onion, diced

2 (12-oz.) cans fat-free, low-sodium chicken broth, *divided*

1½ cups low-fat buttermilk biscuit and baking mix

Pepper (optional)

1. Combine chicken, vegetables, onion, and chicken broth (reserve ½ cup plus 1 tablespoon broth) in slow cooker.

2. Cover and cook on high 2 hours.

3. Combine biscuit and baking mix with reserved broth in a bowl until moistened. Drop by tablespoonfuls over hot chicken and vegetables.

4. Cover and cook on high 10 minutes.

5. Uncover and cook on high 20 minutes more. Sprinkle with pepper, if desired.

NOTE

For a less brothy stew, add another ½ pound of vegetables.

Creamy Cooker Chicken

Makes 6 servings

Ideal slow cooker: 4- to 5-qt.

1 (1-oz.) envelope dry onion soup mix

2 cups sour cream

1 (10¾-oz.) can cream of mushroom soup

6 boneless, skinless chicken breast halves

1. Combine soup mix, sour cream, and cream of mushroom soup in slow cooker. Add chicken, pushing it down so it is submerged in the sauce.

2. Cover and cook on high 1 hour and then on low 6 hours.

Serving suggestion:
Serve over rice or noodles.

Chicken Cacciatore

Makes 6 servings

Ideal slow cooker: 5-qt.

3 lb. bone-in chicken pieces, skin removed

2 green bell peppers, thinly sliced

2 medium onions, thinly sliced

2 garlic cloves, thinly sliced

½ lb. fresh mushrooms, sliced

3 cups chopped tomatoes

1 cup tomato sauce

3 oz. tomato paste

1 Tbsp. balsamic vinegar

1 tsp. salt

1 tsp. dried oregano

½ tsp. dried rosemary

½ tsp. dried basil

¼ tsp. freshly ground black pepper

Hot cooked spaghetti

1 (2-oz.) can sliced black olives, drained

1. Place chicken in slow cooker. Add peppers, onions, garlic, and mushrooms.

2. Combine tomatoes and next 8 ingredients in a small bowl. Pour over vegetables and chicken.

3. Cover and cook on low 5 to 6 hours or until chicken is tender.

4. Serve chicken and sauce over spaghetti in pasta bowls. Sprinkle with olives.

Italian Sausage Dinner

Makes 6 servings

Ideal slow cooker: 4-qt.

1½ lb. Italian sausage, cut into ¾-inch slices

2 Tbsp. steak sauce

1 (28-oz.) can diced Italian-style tomatoes

2 green bell peppers, chopped

½ tsp. dried crushed red pepper (optional)

2 cups uncooked Minute Rice

1. Cook sausage in a large skillet over medium-high heat until browned. Drain well.

2. Place browned sausage and remaining ingredients except rice in slow cooker.

3. Cover and cook on low 8 hours.

4. Stir in uncooked rice. Cover and cook 20 minutes more.

Slow-Cooker Lasagna

Makes 6–8 servings

Ideal slow cooker: 4-qt.

I lb. ground beef, browned

4–5 cups spaghetti sauce, depending on how firm or juicy you like the finished lasagna

I (24-oz.) container cottage cheese

I egg

8–10 lasagna noodles, uncooked

2–3 cups mozzarella cheese

1. Combine ground beef and spaghetti sauce in a bowl.

2. Combine cottage cheese and egg in a bowl.

3. Layer half each of the ground beef mixture, the uncooked noodles, the cottage cheese mixture, and the mozzarella cheese in slow cooker. Repeat layers.

4. Cover and cook on high 4 to 5 hours or on low 6 to 8 hours.

Spaghetti and Meat Sauce

Makes 6–8 servings

Ideal slow cooker: 3- to 4-qt.

1 lb. ground beef

1 Tbsp. vegetable oil

½ lb. fresh mushrooms, sliced

1 medium onion, chopped

3 garlic cloves, minced

½ tsp. dried oregano

½ tsp. salt

1 (6-oz.) can tomato paste

2 (15-oz.) cans tomato sauce

1 (14½-oz.) can petite-cut diced tomatoes

¼ cup freshly grated Parmesan or Romano cheese

1. Brown ground beef in oil in a skillet over medium-high heat. Reserve drippings and transfer meat to slow cooker.

2. Sauté mushrooms, onion, and garlic in drippings until onions are transparent. Add to slow cooker.

3. Add remaining ingredients except cheese to slow cooker. Mix well.

4. Cover and cook on low 6 hours.

5. Sprinkle with cheese.

Serving suggestion:

Serve with pasta and garlic bread.

Tortellini with Broccoli

Makes 4 servings

Ideal slow cooker: 4-qt.

½ cup water

1 (26-oz.) jar of your favorite pasta sauce

1 Tbsp. dried Italian seasoning

1 (9-oz.) pkg. fresh mixed cheese tortellini

1 (16-oz.) pkg. frozen broccoli florets

Grated Parmesan cheese (optional)

1. Combine water, pasta sauce, and Italian seasoning in a bowl.

2. Pour one-third of sauce into slow cooker. Top with tortellini.

3. Pour one-third of sauce over tortellini. Top with broccoli.

4. Pour remaining sauce over broccoli.

5. Cover and cook on high 1½ to 2 hours or until broccoli and pasta are tender but not mushy. Garnish with Parmesan cheese, if desired.

Smothered Pork Chops

Makes 4 servings

Ideal slow cooker: 2-qt.

4 center-cut pork chops

1 (10¾-oz.) can cream
of mushroom soup

1 cup milk

2 Tbsp. dry sherry

2 green onions, chopped

1. Place chops in slow cooker.

2. Combine remaining ingredients in a bowl. Pour over chops.

3. Cover and cook on high 1 hour and then on low 4 to 6 hours or until meat is tender but not dry.

Variation:

Season pork chops with salt and pepper to taste before placing them in the slow cooker in Step 1.

Balsamic-Glazed Pork Ribs

Makes 6–8 servings

Ideal slow cooker: 6-qt.

2 Tbsp. olive oil

I Tbsp. kosher salt

I Tbsp. fennel seeds

I tsp. freshly ground black pepper

I tsp. paprika

½ tsp. dried sage

½ tsp. dried rosemary

¼ tsp. dried thyme

¼–I tsp. dried crushed red pepper

½ tsp. ground coriander

¼ tsp. ground allspice

3 lb. pork ribs

3 Tbsp. balsamic vinegar

1. Combine first 11 ingredients in a small bowl.

2. Rub spice mixture over ribs. Let stand at room temperature 1 hour or refrigerate overnight.

3. Place ribs in slow cooker, cutting to fit if needed.

4. Cover and cook on low 4 to 6 hours or until tender.

5. Preheat broiler.

6. Transfer ribs to a rimmed baking sheet. Brush meaty side of ribs with vinegar and broil 6 inches from heat until browned, about 2 minutes. Let stand 5 minutes. To serve, cut between ribs or serve in slabs.

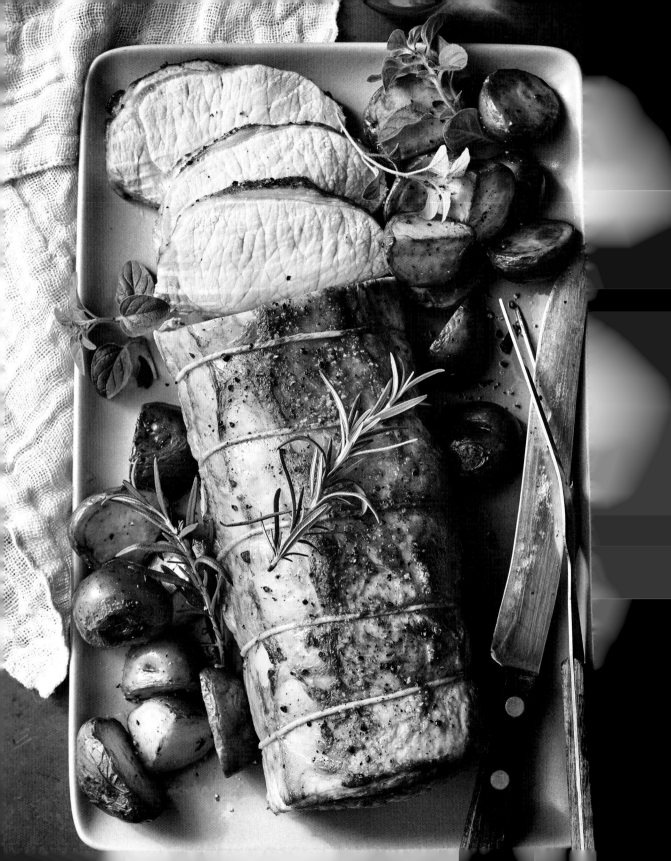

Rosemary Pork Loin

Makes 8–10 servings

Ideal slow cooker: 5-qt.

4–5 lb. pork loin roast

2 cups apple cider

2 garlic cloves, minced

1 Tbsp. fresh rosemary leaves or 1 tsp. dried rosemary

1 tsp. onion salt

¾ tsp. chopped fresh oregano or ¼ tsp. dried oregano

1 bay leaf

1. Place pork loin in a baking pan.

2. Combine remaining ingredients in a bowl. Pour over pork. Cover and refrigerate at least 8 hours, spooning marinade over pork 2 to 3 times if possible.

3. Transfer pork to slow cooker. Pour marinade over pork. Cover and cook on low 3 to 4 hours or until meat registers 145°F on an instant-read thermometer when inserted into center of pork.

4. Transfer pork to a platter. Cover with foil and let stand 15 minutes. Slice pork and serve with cooked marinade, discarding bay leaf.

Ribs with Apples and Kraut

Makes 7 servings

Ideal slow cooker: 6-qt.

1½ lb. pork ribs, trimmed of fat

½ tsp. salt

¼–½ tsp. pepper

½ cup water, apple juice, or white wine (optional)

2 (16-oz.) cans or 1 (2-lb.) bag sauerkraut, undrained

3 medium onions, sliced into rings

2 (8-oz.) cans mushrooms, drained

3 large apples, cored and cut into wedges

⅓ cup brown sugar

½ tsp. celery seed

1. Brown ribs on both sides in a nonstick skillet. Season with salt and pepper.

2. Place ribs in slow cooker. Deglaze skillet with ½ cup water, apple juice, or white wine, if desired. Set drippings aside.

3. In a large bowl, mix together sauerkraut, onions, mushrooms, apple wedges, brown sugar, and celery seed. Spoon over ribs. Pour any reserved drippings over top.

4. Cover and cook on high 3 to 4 hours or on low 7 to 9 hours.

Southwestern Flair

Makes 8–12 servings

Ideal slow cooker: 4-qt.

3–4 lb. chuck roast or flank steak
1 (1¼-oz.) envelope taco seasoning
1 cup chopped onions
1 Tbsp. white vinegar
1¼ cups green chilies

1. Combine meat, taco seasoning, onions, vinegar, and chilies in slow cooker.

2. Cover and cook on high 1 hour. Turn temperature to low and continue cooking 8 hours more.

3. Shred meat with fork.

Serving suggestion:

Serve with tortillas and your choice of salsa, shredded cheese, refried beans, shredded lettuce, chopped tomatoes, and sour cream.

Savory Pepper Steak

Makes 6 servings

Ideal slow cooker: 3-qt.

1 ½ lb. beef round steak (½-inch-thick)

¼ cup all-purpose flour

½ tsp. salt

⅛ tsp. pepper

1 medium onion, chopped or sliced

1 garlic clove, minced

2 large green bell peppers, cut into ½-inch strips, *divided*

1 (29-oz.) can whole tomatoes

1 Tbsp. beef flavor base or 1 beef bouillon cube

1 Tbsp. soy sauce

2 tsp. Worcestershire sauce

3 Tbsp. all-purpose flour

3 Tbsp. water

1. Cut beef into strips.

2. Combine ¼ cup flour, salt, and pepper in a bowl. Toss with beef until well coated. Place in slow cooker.

3. Add onion, garlic, and half the bell pepper slices. Mix well.

4. Combine tomatoes, beef base, soy sauce, and Worcestershire sauce in a bowl. Pour into slow cooker.

5. Cover and cook on high 1 hour and then on low 5 to 7 hours.

6. Turn slow cooker to high and stir in remaining bell pepper.

7. Combine 3 tablespoons flour and 3 tablespoons water to make smooth paste. Stir into slow cooker. Cover and cook 1 hour more or until thickened.

8. Serve over rice.

Home-Style Beef Cubes

Makes 8–10 servings

Ideal slow cooker: 6-qt. oval

½ cup all-purpose flour

I tsp. salt

⅛ tsp. pepper

4 lb. beef cubes

½ cup chopped shallots
or green onions

2 (4-oz.) cans sliced mushrooms,
drained, or ½ lb. fresh mushrooms,
sliced

I (14½-oz.) can beef broth

I tsp. Worcestershire sauce

2 tsp. ketchup

¼ cup water

3 Tbsp. all-purpose flour

Cooked egg noodles

Garnish: fresh parsley

1. Combine ½ cup flour, salt, and pepper. Toss beef in flour mixture to coat, shaking off excess. Place in slow cooker.

2. Cover with shallots or green onions, and mushrooms.

3. Combine broth, Worcestershire sauce, and ketchup. Pour into slow cooker. Mix well. Cover and cook on low 8 hours.

4. One hour before serving, stir together ¼ cup water and 3 tablespoons flour to make a smooth paste. Add into slow cooker, stirring constantly to blend. Cover and cook until broth thickens. Serve over hot buttered noodles. Garnish, if desired.

Beefy Slow-Cooker Spaghetti

Makes 3 quarts

Ideal slow cooker: 6-qt.

3- to 3½-lb. boneless chuck roast, trimmed and cut in half

2 tsp. salt, *divided*

2 Tbsp. olive oil

2 garlic cloves, minced

1 large onion, chopped

4 (14½-oz.) cans Italian-style diced tomatoes, undrained

1 (15-oz.) can tomato sauce

1 (12-oz.) can tomato paste

1 Tbsp. sugar

2 tsp. dried basil

2 tsp. dried oregano

1 tsp. dried crushed red pepper

Hot cooked spaghetti (optional)

1. Sprinkle roast evenly with 1 teaspoon salt. Cook roast in hot oil in a large skillet over medium-high heat 3 minutes on each side or until browned.

2. Combine minced garlic, next 8 ingredients, and remaining 1 teaspoon salt, in slow cooker; gently add roast.

3. Cover and cook on high 6 hours or until roast is very tender.

4. Remove roast from slow cooker and shred using two forks. Skim off any fat from tomato sauce, if desired, and return shredded meat to sauce. Serve over hot cooked spaghetti, if desired.

TIP

This makes enough sauce for several meals, so serve some when it's first made and freeze the rest in airtight containers for up to 6 weeks, if desired.

Angel Chicken Pasta

Makes 4 servings

Ideal slow cooker: 4- to 5-qt.

¼ cup butter

1 (0.7-oz.) envelope dry Italian salad dressing mix

½ cup dry white wine

1 (10¾-oz.) can golden mushroom soup

½ (8-oz.) container cream cheese with chives

4 boneless, skinless chicken breast halves

1. Melt butter in a large saucepan over low heat. Stir in salad dressing mix. Add wine and soup, stirring to blend. Add cream cheese and stir until smooth. Do not boil.

2. Arrange chicken in slow cooker. Pour sauce over top.

3. Cover and cook on low 5 to 6 hours or just until chicken is tender but not dry.

Serving suggestion:

About 10 minutes before serving, cook pasta. Serve chicken and sauce over pasta.

Chicken in Wine

Makes 4–6 servings

Ideal slow cooker: 4-qt.

2 lb. chicken breasts or pieces, trimmed of skin and fat

1 (10¾-oz. can) 98% fat-free, reduced-sodium cream of mushroom soup

1 (10¾-oz.) can French onion soup

1 cup dry white wine or chicken broth

1. Place chicken in slow cooker.

2. Combine soups and wine. Pour over chicken.

3. Cover and cook on high 1 hour and then on low 4 to 6 hours.

4. Serve over rice, pasta, or potatoes.

Chicken Casablanca

Makes 6–8 servings

Ideal slow cooker: 4- or 5-qt.

2 large onions, sliced

1 tsp. ground ginger

3 garlic cloves, minced

2 Tbsp. canola oil

3 large carrots, diced

2 large potatoes, unpeeled, diced

3 lb. skinless chicken pieces

½ tsp. ground cumin

½ tsp. salt

½ tsp. pepper

¼ tsp. ground cinnamon

2 Tbsp. raisins

1 (14½-oz.) can chopped tomatoes

3 small zucchini, sliced

1 (15-oz.) can garbanzo beans, drained

2 Tbsp. chopped fresh parsley

1. Sauté onions, ginger, and garlic in oil in a skillet over low heat. Place onion mixture in slow cooker, reserving oil. Sauté carrots and potatoes in oil. Place in slow cooker, reserving oil.

2. Brown chicken in reserved oil over medium heat. Place in slow cooker. Mix gently with vegetables.

3. Combine seasonings in a separate bowl. Sprinkle over chicken and vegetables. Add raisins and tomatoes.

4. Cover and cook on high 4 to 6 hours.

5. Add sliced zucchini, beans, and parsley 30 minutes before serving.

6. Serve over cooked rice or couscous.

Variation:

Add ½ teaspoon turmeric and ¼ teaspoon cayenne pepper to Step 3.

Tex-Mex Chicken Rollups

Makes 6 servings

Ideal slow cooker: 5- to 6-qt. oval

6 boneless, skinless chicken breast halves (about 1½ lb.)

6 oz. Monterey Jack cheese, cut into 2-inch-long, ½-inch-thick sticks

2 (4-oz.) cans chopped green chilies, drained

¾ cup all-purpose flour

½ cup butter, melted

½ cup dry bread crumbs

¼ cup grated Parmesan cheese

1 Tbsp. chili powder

½ tsp. salt

½ tsp. ground cumin

Pinch cayenne pepper (optional)

1. Place chicken on a cutting board. Cover with plastic wrap and flatten each to ⅛-inch thickness using a mallet.

2. Place a cheese stick in middle of each and top with a mound of chilies. Roll up and tuck in ends. Secure with toothpick. Set aside.

3. Place flour in a shallow dish and melted butter in another. In another dish, combine bread crumbs, Parmesan cheese, chili powder, salt, cumin, and cayenne, if desired.

4. Dip each chicken roll in flour, butter, and crumb mixture. Place seam-side down in a single layer in greased slow cooker.

5. Cover and cook on low 4 to 4½ hours or until chicken registers 165°F on a meat thermometer.

6. Preheat broiler.

7. Transfer chicken to a rimmed baking sheet. Place under broiler until crumbs are crispy and lightly browned. Remove toothpicks before serving.

Creamy Salmon and Wheat Berries

Makes 5 servings

Ideal slow cooker: 3½-qt.

2 cups fat-free chicken broth

2 cups water

1 (10-oz.) pkg. frozen corn

1 cup chopped celery

½ cup chopped onion

¾ cup wheat berries

1 (8-oz.) pkg. fat-free cream cheese, cut into cubes

1 (16-oz.) can salmon, drained, skin and bones removed, and coarsely flaked

1 Tbsp. fresh dill weed

1. Combine chicken broth, water, corn, celery, onion, and wheat berries in slow cooker.

2. Cover and cook on high 3½ to 4 hours or on low 8 to 10 hours.

3. Turn slow cooker to high. Add cheese, stirring until melted.

4. Gently stir in salmon and dill.

5. Cover and cook 10 minutes more.

Cajun Catfish

Makes 4 servings

Ideal slow cooker: 5- to 6-qt. oval

I Tbsp. butter

½ cup finely chopped green onions

2 garlic cloves, pressed

I cup sweet white wine

4 (6-oz.) catfish fillets (½-inch-thick)

I ½ tsp. Creole seasoning (we used Tony Chachere's)

Thinly sliced green onions

1. Melt butter in small saucepan over medium-high heat. Add green onions and garlic; sauté 1 minute or until tender. Add wine and simmer 10 to 13 minutes or until mixture is reduced by half.

2. Sprinkle fish with Creole seasoning. Place fish in slow cooker coated with cooking spray.

3. Carefully pour wine mixture around fish in slow cooker. Cover and cook on low 45 minutes to 1 hour or until fish flakes easily when tested with a fork.

Sage Turkey Thighs

Makes 4 servings

Ideal slow cooker: 3-qt.

4 medium carrots, halved

1 medium onion, chopped

¾ cup water, *divided*

1½ tsp. dried sage, *divided*

2 skinless turkey thighs
or drumsticks (about 2 lb.)

1 Tbsp. cornstarch

1. Combine carrots, onion, ½ cup water, and 1 teaspoon sage in slow cooker. Place turkey on top and sprinkle with remaining sage.

2. Cover and cook on high 1 hour and then on low 4 to 6 hours or until a meat thermometer reads 180°F.

3. Remove turkey and vegetables to a serving platter. Cover to keep warm.

4. Pour cooking juices into a saucepan and bring to a boil.

5. Combine cornstarch and remaining ¼ cup water in a small bowl, stirring until smooth. Stir into boiling juices. Cook 2 minutes or until thickened, stirring constantly. Serve over turkey and vegetables.

Variation:

Add 1 teaspoon minced garlic in Step 1. For a more flavorful gravy, add 1 teaspoon browning sauce, ¼ teaspoon salt, and ⅛ teaspoon pepper to the boiling cooking juices before adding the cornstarch mixture in Step 5.

Veggie Mains

Corn Bread-Topped Frijoles

Makes 8–10 servings

Ideal slow cooker: 5-qt.

1 medium onion, chopped

1 medium green bell pepper, chopped

1 Tbsp. vegetable oil

2 garlic cloves, minced

1 (16-oz.) can kidney beans, rinsed and drained

1 (15-oz.) can pinto beans, rinsed and drained

1 (14½-oz.) can diced tomatoes, undrained

1 (8-oz.) can tomato sauce

1 tsp. chili powder

½ tsp. pepper

¼ tsp. hot pepper sauce

Garnish: sour cream, sliced green onions

Corn Bread Topping:

½ cup all-purpose flour

½ cup yellow cornmeal

2 tsp. sugar

1 tsp. baking powder

¼ tsp. salt

1 egg, lightly beaten

¾ cup skim milk

½ cup cream-style corn

1 Tbsp. vegetable oil

1. Sauté onion and bell pepper in oil in a large skillet over medium-high heat until tender. Add garlic; cook 1 minute more. Transfer to greased slow cooker.

2. Stir in beans, tomatoes, tomato sauce, chili powder, pepper, and hot pepper sauce.

3. Cover and cook on high 1 hour.

4. Meanwhile, combine flour, cornmeal, sugar, baking powder, and salt in a large bowl.

5. Combine egg, milk, corn, and oil in a small bowl. Add to flour mixture and stir well. Spoon evenly over bean mixture.

6. Cover and cook on high 2 hours more or until a toothpick inserted near center of corn bread comes out clean. Garnish, if desired. Serve with corn chips.

"Baked" Ziti

Makes 8–10 servings

Ideal slow cooker: 5-qt.

1 (16-oz.) container cottage cheese

1 Tbsp. Parmesan cheese

1 egg

1 tsp. parsley flakes

1 tsp. dried minced garlic

⅛ tsp. pepper

⅛ tsp. salt

1 (45-oz.) jar spaghetti sauce, *divided*

1 (14-oz.) jar spaghetti sauce, *divided*

1 lb. uncooked ziti

8 oz. mozzarella cheese, shredded

1. Combine first 7 ingredients in a bowl, stirring well.

2. Place 2 cups spaghetti sauce in greased slow cooker and top with one-third of uncooked pasta. Spoon one-third of cottage cheese mixture over pasta.

3. Repeat layers two more times. Spoon remaining 1 cup spaghetti sauce over top.

4. Cover and cook on low 3½ hours. Sprinkle mozzarella cheese over top and cook, uncovered, 30 minutes more. Let stand 15 minutes before serving.

Lentil-Rice Salad Bowl

Makes 4–6 servings

Ideal slow cooker: 5-qt.

I cup brown lentils, rinsed

I cup uncooked brown long grain rice

I onion, chopped

3½ cups water, vegetable broth,
or combination

I tsp. salt

¼ tsp. freshly ground black pepper

½ tsp. ground cumin

I bay leaf

Salad:

2 Tbsp. fresh lemon juice

½ tsp. grated lemon peel

2 Tbsp. olive oil

½ tsp. salt

2 small cucumbers, diced

2 medium tomatoes, diced

3 green onions, sliced

⅓ cup chopped fresh basil

½ cup crumbled feta cheese

1. Combine lentils and next 7 ingredients in slow cooker.

2. Cover and cook on high 3 to 4 hours or until lentils and rice are tender but not mushy. Remove bay leaf.

3. For salad, combine lemon juice, peel, olive oil, and salt in a medium bowl, whisking well.

4. Add cucumbers, tomatoes, green onions, basil, and cheese to bowl and toss gently.

5. To serve, place a scoop of lentil rice mixture in each soup bowl. Top with a scoop of the salad.

TIP

Keep the rice mixture in slow cooker while you prepare the salad topping. The salad will wilt if it sits in its dressing too long.

Arroz Con Queso

Makes 6–8 servings

Ideal slow cooker: 4-qt.

1 (14½-oz.) can whole tomatoes, mashed

1 (15-oz.) can Mexican-style beans, undrained

1½ cups uncooked long-grain rice

1 cup grated Monterey Jack cheese

1 large onion, finely chopped

1 cup cottage cheese

1 (4¼-oz.) can chopped green chili peppers, drained

1 Tbsp. vegetable oil

3 garlic cloves, minced

1 tsp. salt

1 cup shredded Monterey Jack cheese

1. Combine all ingredients except final cup of cheese in well-greased slow cooker.

2. Cover. Cook on low 6 to 9 hours, or until rice is fully cooked but dish is not dry. Sprinkle with remaining cheese before serving.

Serving suggestion:

Serve with chips and salsa on the side.

Chilies Rellenos

Makes 6–8 servings

Ideal slow cooker: 6-qt.

1 (8-oz.) can whole green or red chilies

½–1 lb. Monterey Jack cheese, cut into 1-inch-wide, 3-inch-long, ¼-inch-thick strips

4 large eggs

¼ cup all-purpose flour

1¼ cups milk

½ tsp. salt

Pepper to taste

⅓ cup shredded sharp cheddar cheese

Paprika

1. Rinse seeds from chilies. Spread chilies in single layer on paper towel. Carefully pat dry.

2. Split each chili open and insert strips of cheese.

3. Beat eggs at medium speed with an electric mixer. Gradually add flour, beating until smooth. Add milk, salt, and pepper. Beat thoroughly.

4. Arrange stuffed chilies in a shallow grease baking pan that fits into slow cooker. Sprinkle with cheddar cheese and paprika. Gently pour egg mixture over all.

5. Place pan on small trivet or metal jar rings in slow cooker. Prop the slow cooker lid open at one end with a wooden spoon handle. Cook on high 3½ to 4½ hours or until set and bubbling at edges.

Meatless Shepherd's Pie

Makes 6 servings

Ideal slow cooker: 4-qt.

2 (2-oz.) pkg. frozen meatless burger crumbles

2 Tbsp. all-purpose flour

1 (14½-oz.) can diced tomatoes with basil, garlic, and oregano, undrained

1 (16-oz.) pkg. frozen peas and carrots

1 tsp. dried minced onion

1 (24-oz.) pkg. refrigerated sour cream and chive mashed potatoes

1 cup shredded sharp cheddar cheese

Garnish: chopped fresh chives

1. Toss together burger crumbles and flour in a large bowl until crumbles are coated.

2. Stir in tomatoes, peas and carrots, and onion. Spoon mixture into lightly greased slow cooker.

3. Microwave potatoes at high 1 minute according to pkg. directions. Stir and spread over vegetable mixture in slow cooker.

4. Cover and cook on low 4 hours. Turn heat to high. Sprinkle cheese over potatoes.

5. Cover and cook 7 minutes or until cheese is melted. Garnish, if desired.

Mediterranean Eggplant

Makes 8 servings

Ideal slow cooker: 5-qt.

1 medium-size red onion, chopped

2 garlic cloves, crushed

1 cup fresh mushrooms, sliced

2 Tbsp. olive oil

1 eggplant, unpeeled and cubed

2 green bell peppers, coarsely chopped

1 (28-oz.) can crushed tomatoes, undrained

1 (28-oz.) can garbanzo beans, rinsed and drained

2 Tbsp. minced fresh rosemary

1 cup fresh parsley, chopped

½ cup kalamata olives, pitted and sliced

1. Spray slow cooker with cooking spray.

2. Sauté onion, garlic, and mushrooms in olive oil in a skillet over medium heat. Transfer to slow cooker.

3. Add eggplant, peppers, tomatoes, garbanzos, rosemary, and parsley.

4. Cover and cook on low 5 to 6 hours.

5. Stir in sliced olives just before serving.

6. Serve mixture with couscous or polenta.

Greek Eggplant Bake

Makes 6–8 servings

Ideal slow cooker: 4-qt.

½ cup chopped onion

½ cup chopped green bell pepper

½ cup sliced mushrooms

2 tsp. olive oil

2 (8-oz.) cans tomato sauce

I tsp. Worcestershire sauce

I Tbsp. brown sugar

1½ tsp. dried oregano

I tsp. minced garlic

½ tsp. salt

½ cup chopped fresh parsley

I medium eggplant, peeled or unpeeled, cut into ⅛-inch slices, *divided*

1½ cups shredded mozzarella cheese, *divided*

¼ cup sliced black olives

1. Sauté onion, bell pepper, and mushrooms in oil in a large skillet over medium-high heat.

2. Stir in tomato sauce, Worcestershire sauce, brown sugar, oregano, garlic, salt, and parsley.

3. Layer half the tomato sauce mixture, half the eggplant, and half the cheese in slow cooker.

4. Repeat layers, ending with cheese. Sprinkle with olives. Cover and cook on high 2 to 2½ hours or on low 4 to 5 hours.

Tempeh-Stuffed Peppers

Makes 4 servings

Ideal slow cooker: 5-qt.

4 oz. tempeh, cubed

1 garlic clove, minced

1 (28-oz.) can crushed tomatoes, *divided*

2 tsp. soy sauce

¼ cup chopped onions

1½ cups cooked rice

2 cups shredded cheese of your choice, *divided*

Tabasco sauce to taste

4 green, red, or yellow bell peppers, tops removed and seeded

1. Steam tempeh, 10 minutes in saucepan. Mash in bowl with the garlic, half the tomatoes, and soy sauce.

2. Stir in onions, rice, 1½ cups cheese, and Tabasco sauce, if desired. Stuff mixture into peppers.

3. Place peppers in slow cooker, 3 on bottom and 1 on top. Pour remaining half of tomatoes over peppers.

4. Cover. Cook on low 6 to 8 hours. Top with remaining ½ cup cheese in last 30 minutes.

Easy Stuffed Shells

Makes 7 servings

Ideal slow cooker: 4-qt.

1 (20-oz.) bag frozen stuffed shells, thawed

1 (15-oz.) can marinara or spaghetti sauce

1 (15-oz.) can green beans, drained

1. Place shells around edge of greased slow cooker. Cover with marinara sauce.

2. Pour green beans in center.

3. Cover and cook on high 3 hours or on low 8 hours.

Serving suggestion:

Serve with garlic toast and salad.

Variation:

Reverse Steps 2 and 3. Double the amount of marinara sauce and pour over both the shells and the beans.

Spinach Casserole

Makes 6 servings

Ideal slow cooker: 2½-qt.

2 (10-oz.) pkg. frozen spinach, thawed
and drained

2 cups white sauce, or cottage cheese

¼ cup butter, cubed

1¼ cups American cheese,
cut into squares

2 eggs, beaten

¼ cup flour

1 tsp. salt

1 garlic clove or ¼ tsp. garlic powder

1. Combine all ingredients. Mix well. Pour into greased slow cooker.

2. Cover. Cook on high for 1 hour. Reduce heat to low and cook 4 to 5 hours.

Cabbage Casserole

Makes 6 servings

Ideal slow cooker: 4- to 5-qt.

1 large head cabbage, chopped

2 cups water

1 Tbsp. salt

⅓ cup butter

¼ cup flour

½–1 tsp. salt

¼ tsp. pepper

1⅓ cups milk

1⅓ cups shredded cheddar cheese

1. Cook cabbage in saucepan in boiling water and salt for 5 minutes. Drain. Place in slow cooker.

2. In saucepan, melt butter. Stir in flour, salt, and pepper. Add milk, stirring constantly on low heat for 5 minutes. Remove from heat. Stir in cheese. Pour over cabbage.

3. Cover. Cook on low 4 to 5 hours.

Variation:

Replace cabbage with cauliflower.

White Bean Casserole

Makes 6–8 servings

Ideal slow cooker: 4- to 5-qt.

2 cups dried white beans

8 cups water

4 medium onions, chopped or thinly sliced

4 tsp. olive oil, *divided*

½ tsp. salt

¼ tsp. pepper

2 Tbsp. chopped fresh or 2 tsp. dried basil

2 Tbsp. chopped fresh or 2 tsp. dried parsley

1 Tbsp. fresh or 1 tsp. dried thyme

4 slices toasted bread

2 Tbsp. butter, cut into pieces

1. Place dried beans in a stockpot. Cover with 8 cups water. Cover pot with lid. Let beans soak 8 hours or overnight.

2. Drain beans. Place in greased slow cooker. Stir in onions, 1 teaspoon oil, salt, and pepper. Cover and cook on high 4 to 5 hours or on low 9 to 10 hours, until beans are tender but still hold their shape. Stir in basil, parsley, and thyme 30 minutes before end of cooking time.

3. Process toast and 1 tablespoon olive oil in a food processor to make bread crumbs. Sprinkle over bean mixture. Top with butter. Cook, uncovered, on high 20 to 30 minutes more.

Cheesy Macaroni

Makes 10–12 servings

Ideal slow cooker: 6-qt.

1 lb. uncooked macaroni

1 (12-oz.) can evaporated milk

3 cups milk

2 lb. pasteurized prepared cheese product, cubed, or shredded sharp cheddar cheese

1. Cook macaroni according to package directions. Drain.

2. Combine remaining ingredients in slow cooker.

3. Stir in cooked macaroni.

4. Cover and cook on low 3 hours.

Variation:

Add ¼ cup finely chopped onion, ¼ teaspoon chili powder, or 1½ teaspoon Worcestershire sauce. Garnish with chopped fresh parsley, chives, or green and/or red bell pepper just before serving.

Pesto Lasagna

Makes 8 servings

Ideal slow cooker: 6-qt. oval

4 cups torn fresh spinach

2 cups sliced cremini mushrooms

½ cup pesto

1¾ cups shredded mozzarella cheese, *divided*

¾ cup shredded provolone cheese

1 (15-oz.) container ricotta cheese

1 large egg, lightly beaten

¾ cup freshly grated Parmesan cheese, *divided*

1 (26-oz.) jar tomato-basil pasta sauce

1 (8-oz.) can tomato sauce

1 (8-oz.) pkg. no-boil lasagna noodles

1. Steam spinach, covered, 3 minutes or until spinach wilts. Drain, squeeze dry, and coarsely chop. Combine spinach, mushrooms, and pesto in a medium bowl, and set aside.

2. Combine ¾ cup mozzarella, provolone, ricotta, and egg. Stir in ¼ cup Parmesan cheese, and set aside. Combine pasta sauce and tomato sauce.

3. Spread 1 cup pasta sauce mixture in bottom of slow cooker coated with cooking spray. Arrange 3 noodles over pasta sauce mixture and top with 1 cup cheese mixture and 1 cup spinach mixture. Repeat layers once, ending with remaining 1 cup spinach mixture. Arrange 3 noodles over spinach mixture; top with remaining cheese mixture and 1 cup pasta sauce mixture. Place 3 noodles over sauce mixture; spread remaining sauce mixture over noodles. Sprinkle with remaining ½ cup Parmesan cheese and remaining 1 cup mozzarella cheese. Cover and cook on low 5 hours or until done.

Taco Twist

Makes 6–8 servings

Ideal slow cooker: 3- to 4-qt.

1 medium onion, chopped

2 garlic cloves, minced

2 Tbsp. canola or olive oil

3 cups reduced-sodium vegetable broth

1 (15-oz.) can black beans, rinsed and drained

1 (14½-oz.) can diced tomatoes, undrained

1½ cups picante sauce

1 cup spiral pasta, uncooked

1 small green bell pepper, chopped

2 tsp. chili powder

1 tsp. ground cumin

½ cup shredded reduced-fat cheese

Guacamole (optional)

1. Sauté onion and garlic in oil in a skillet.

2. Combine all ingredients except cheese and guacamole in slow cooker.

3. Cover and cook on low 3 hours or just until pasta is tender.

4. Serve with cheese and, if desired, guacamole.

Polenta-and-Mushroom Alfredo Lasagna

Makes 6 servings

Ideal slow cooker: 6-qt.

2 (3½-oz.) pkg. fresh shiitake mushrooms

I (8-oz.) pkg. sliced fresh button mushrooms

I medium onion, cut in half crosswise and sliced vertically

3 Tbsp. olive oil

2 (16-oz.) jars Alfredo sauce (we used Classico)

¼ cup dry white wine

½ tsp. freshly ground pepper

¼ tsp. ground nutmeg

2 (17-oz.) tubes pesto-flavored or plain polenta, cut into ½-inch slices (we used Marjon Basil and Garlic Polenta)

I cup freshly grated Parmesan cheese

1. Remove and discard stems from shiitake mushrooms; thinly slice mushrooms. Sauté mushrooms and onion in hot oil in a large skillet over medium-high heat until onion is tender and liquid is absorbed.

2. Whisk together Alfredo sauce, wine, pepper, and nutmeg in a bowl; stir into mushroom mixture. Spread 3 tablespoons mushroom mixture in slow cooker. Layer one-third of polenta slices over sauce. Sprinkle ½ cup Parmesan cheese over polenta; top with half of remaining mushroom mixture. Layer one-third of polenta slices and remaining half of mushroom mixture; top with remaining one-third of polenta slices. Sprinkle with remaining ½ cup Parmesan cheese.

3. Cover and cook on low 4 hours or until set. Remove lid and let lasagna stand 15 minutes before serving.

Easy Vegetable Pot Pie

Makes 5 servings

Ideal slow cooker: 5-qt.

8 small red potatoes, peeled and diced

3 carrots, chopped

2 celery ribs, chopped

1 cup sliced fresh mushrooms

1 tsp. pepper

½ tsp. celery salt

¼ tsp. salt

2 (10¾-oz.) cans cream of mushroom soup

1¼ cups frozen mixed vegetables

5 hot cooked biscuits

Garnish: chopped fresh basil

1. Combine all ingredients except biscuits and garnish in slow cooker coated with cooking spray.

2. Cover and cook on low 5 hours. Spoon vegetable mixture into bowls. Top with biscuits. Garnish, if desired.

Wild Mushrooms Italian

Makes 4–5 servings

Ideal slow cooker: 3- to 4-qt.

2 large onions, chopped

3 large red bell peppers, chopped

3 large green bell peppers, chopped

2–3 Tbsp. vegetable oil

1 (12-oz.) pkg. oyster mushrooms, cleaned and chopped

4 garlic cloves, minced

3 fresh bay leaves

10 fresh basil leaves, chopped

1 Tbsp. salt

1½ tsp. pepper

1 (28-oz.) can Italian plum tomatoes, crushed or chopped

1. Sauté onion and bell pepper in oil in a skillet until soft. Stir in mushrooms and garlic. Sauté just until mushrooms begin to brown. Pour into slow cooker.

2. Add remaining ingredients to slow cooker. Stir well.

3. Cover and cook on low 6 to 8 hours.

Side Dishes

Green Rice Casserole

Makes 6 servings

Ideal slow cooker: 3½-qt.

1⅓ cups evaporated milk

2 Tbsp. vegetable oil

3 eggs

¼ small onion, minced

½ small carrot, minced (optional)

1 (10-oz.) pkg. frozen chopped spinach, thawed and drained

2 tsp. salt

¼ tsp. pepper

1 cup shredded sharp cheddar cheese

3 cups cooked long-grain rice

1. Beat together milk, oil, and eggs until well combined.

2. Stir in remaining ingredients. Mix well. Pour into greased slow cooker.

3. Cover and cook on high 1 hour. Stir. Then cover and cook on low 4 to 6 hours.

Cheddar Rice

Makes 8–10 servings

Ideal slow cooker: 4-qt.

2 cups uncooked brown rice

3 Tbsp. butter

½ cup thinly sliced green onions or shallots

I tsp. salt

5 cups water

2 cups shredded cheddar cheese

½ tsp. pepper

Additional sliced green onions (optional)

1. Combine rice, butter, green onions or shallots, and salt in slow cooker.

2. Bring 5 cups water to boil in a saucepan and pour over rice mixture.

3. Cover and cook on high 2 to 3 hours or until rice is tender and liquid is absorbed.

4. Stir in cheese 5 minutes before serving.

5. Garnish with pepper and additional green onions, if desired.

Caribbean-Style Rice and Beans

Makes 4 servings

Ideal slow cooker: 4-qt.

1 (15-oz.) can dark red kidney beans, rinsed and drained

1 (14-oz.) can light coconut milk

1 cup long-grain white rice, uncooked

½ cup water

½ tsp. salt

¼ tsp. ground allspice

3 fresh thyme sprigs or 1 tsp. dried thyme

1 garlic clove, sliced

1. Combine all ingredients in slow cooker, stirring gently.

2. Cover and cook on high 2 to 3 hours until rice is tender.

Parmesan Potato Wedges

Makes 6 servings

Ideal slow cooker: 3-qt.

2 lb. small red potatoes, cut into ½-inch wedges

¼ cup chopped onion

2 Tbsp. butter, cut into small pieces

1½ Tbsp. chopped fresh oregano or 1½ tsp. dried oregano

¼ cup freshly grated Parmesan cheese

1. Layer potatoes, onion, butter, and oregano in slow cooker.

2. Cover and cook on high 2 hours or until potatoes are tender.

3. Spoon into serving dish and sprinkle with cheese.

Squash Medley

Makes 8 servings

Ideal slow cooker: 3½-qt.

8 summer squash, or zucchini, each about 4 inches long, peeled or not, thinly sliced, *divided*

½ tsp. salt

2 tomatoes, peeled and chopped, or 1 (14½-oz.) can diced tomatoes, *divided*

½ cup sliced green onions, *divided*

Small green bell pepper, chopped, *divided*

1 chicken bouillon cube

¼ cup hot water

4 slices bacon, fried and crumbled

¼ cup fine dry bread crumbs

1. Sprinkle squash with salt.

2. In slow cooker, layer half the squash, tomatoes, onions, and bell pepper. Repeat layers.

3. Dissolve bouillon in hot water. Pour into slow cooker.

4. Top with bacon. Sprinkle bread crumbs over top.

5. Cover. Cook on low 4 to 6 hours.

Special Green Beans

Makes 12–14 servings

Ideal slow cooker: 4-qt.

4 (14½-oz.) cans green beans, drained

1 (10¾-oz.) can cream of mushroom soup

1 (14½-oz.) can chicken broth

1 cup potato tots

1 (3-oz.) can French-fried onion rings

1. Place green beans in slow cooker.

2. In a bowl, mix together soup and broth. Spread over beans.

3. Spoon potato tots over top. Top with onion rings.

4. Cover and cook on high 1 to 2 hours or until heated through and potatoes are cooked.

Broccoli, Corn, and Onion Gratin

Makes 6 servings

Ideal slow cooker: 4-qt.

1½ cups chopped broccoli

2 cups cream-style corn

2 eggs, lightly beaten

½ cup plain yogurt

1 Tbsp. all-purpose flour

1 tsp. seasoned salt

1 cup French-fried onions, *divided*

1. Place broccoli in greased slow cooker.

2. Combine corn, eggs, yogurt, flour, and seasoned salt in a bowl.

3. Pour half the corn mixture over broccoli. Sprinkle with ½ cup onions.

4. Pour remaining corn mixture over onions. Sprinkle with remaining ½ cup onions.

5. Cover and cook on low 2 to 3 hours, until mixture is set and broccoli is tender.

Fast and Fabulous Brussels Sprouts

Makes 4–6 servings

Ideal slow cooker: 2- or 3-qt.

1 lb. Brussels sprouts, trimmed and halved

3 Tbsp. butter, melted

1½ Tbsp. Dijon mustard

½ tsp. dried tarragon (optional)

¼ tsp. salt

¼ tsp. freshly ground pepper

¼ cup water

Garnish: fresh tarragon

1. Combine all ingredients except garnish in slow cooker.

2. Cover and cook on high 2 to 2½ hours or on low 4 to 5 hours, until sprouts are just tender. Some Brussels sprouts at sides will get brown and crispy.

3. Stir before serving. Garnish with fresh tarragon, if desired.

Sweet-Sour Cabbage

Makes 6 servings

Ideal slow cooker: 6-qt.

I medium head red
or green cabbage, shredded

2 onions, chopped

4 tart apples, peeled and quartered

½ cup raisins

¼ cup lemon juice

¼ cup cider or apple juice

3 Tbsp. honey

I Tbsp. caraway seeds

Dash of allspice

½ tsp. salt

1. Combine all ingredients in slow cooker.

2. Cover and cook on high 3 to 5 hours, or until vegetables are tender.

Quick Broccoli Fix

Makes 6 servings

Ideal slow cooker: 3½-qt.

1 lb. fresh or frozen broccoli, cut up

1 (10¾-oz.) can cream of mushroom soup

½ cup mayonnaise

½ cup plain yogurt

½ lb. sliced fresh mushrooms

1 cup shredded cheddar cheese, *divided*

1 cup crushed saltine crackers

Sliced almonds (optional)

1. Microwave broccoli at high for 3 minutes. Place in greased slow cooker.

2. Combine soup, mayonnaise, yogurt, mushrooms, and ½ cup cheese in a large bowl. Spoon over broccoli and stir together to combine.

3. Cover and cook on low 5 to 6 hours.

4. Top with remaining cheese and crackers during last 30 minutes of cooking.

5. Sprinkle with sliced almonds before serving, if desired.

Make-Ahead Mixed Potato Florentine

Makes 10–12 servings

Ideal slow cooker: 4-qt.

6 medium-sized white potatoes

3 medium-sized sweet potatoes

I large onion, chopped

I–2 garlic cloves, pressed

2 Tbsp. butter

2 Tbsp. olive oil

8 oz. low-fat or non-fat cream cheese, at room temperature

½ cup non-fat sour cream

½ cup non-fat plain yogurt

I tsp. salt, or to taste

1–1 ½ tsp. fresh dill

¼ tsp. black pepper

I (10-oz.) pkg. frozen, chopped spinach, thawed and squeezed dry

1. Peel and quarter both white and sweet potatoes. Place in slow cooker. Barely cover with water.

2. Cover. Cook on low 6 to 8 hours, or until potatoes are falling-apart-tender.

3. Meanwhile, in a saucepan, sauté onion and garlic in butter and olive oil, on low heat, until soft and golden.

4. In an electric mixer bowl, combine sautéed onion and garlic with cream cheese, sour cream, yogurt, salt, dill weed, and pepper. Whip until well blended. Set aside.

5. Drain off some of the potato cooking water, but reserve. Mash potatoes in some of their cooking water until soft and creamy. Add more cooking water if you'd like a creamier result.

6. Stir onion-cheese mixture into mashed potatoes.

7. Fold spinach into potato mixture.

8. Turn into greased 4-quart slow cooker. Cook for 2 hours on low, or until heated through.

9. If you've made the potatoes in advance, refrigerate them until the day of your gathering. Heat potatoes in slow cooker for 3 to 4 hours on low, or until heated through.

Orange-Glazed Sweet Potatoes

Makes 8 servings

Ideal slow cooker: 5-qt.

8 medium sweet potatoes, peeled

½ cup water

½ tsp. salt

1 cup brown sugar, packed

2 Tbsp. cornstarch

½ tsp. grated orange peel

2 cups orange juice

½ cup raisins

6 Tbsp. butter

¼ cup chopped walnuts

1. Arrange sweet potatoes in slow cooker. Add ½ cup water and salt.

2. Cover and cook on low 5 to 8 hours or until potatoes are tender. Discard any remaining water.

3. While potatoes cook, combine brown sugar and cornstarch in a pan. Stir in orange peel, orange juice, and raisins. Cook over medium heat until thickened and bubbly, stirring frequently. Cook 1 minute more.

4. Add butter and walnuts to juice mixture, stirring until butter melts.

5. Remove potatoes. Let cool slightly. Cut potatoes into ½-inch slices.

6. Place layer of potato slices in cooker. Pour half of sauce over top. Make a second layer of potatoes. Top with remaining sauce.

7. Cover and cook on high 1 hour or until potatoes are caramelized and glazed.

Easy Cheesy Potatoes

Makes 4 servings

Ideal slow cooker: 4-qt.

1 (30-oz.) pkg. frozen hash brown potatoes, partially thawed

1 (1-lb.) pkg. kielbasa, chopped

1 medium onion, diced

1 (10¾-oz.) can cheddar cheese soup

1 soup can of milk

1. Spray inside of slow cooker with cooking spray.

2. Place potatoes, kielbasa, and onion in slow cooker. Stir together.

3. Mix soup and milk in a bowl, stirring until well blended. Pour into slow cooker. Stir gently.

4. Cover and cook on high 3 hours or on low 7 to 8 hours.

Fruited Wild Rice with Pecans

Makes 4 servings

Ideal slow cooker: 3-qt.

½ cup chopped onions

2 Tbsp. butter, cut in chunks

1 (6-oz.) pkg. long-grain and wild rice, uncooked

Seasoning packet from wild rice pkg.

1½ cups hot water

⅔ cup apple juice

1 large tart apple, chopped

¼ cup raisins

¼ cup coarsely chopped pecans

1. Combine all ingredients except pecans in greased slow cooker.

2. Cover. Cook on high 2 to 2½ hours, or until rice is fully cooked.

3. Stir in pecans. Serve.

Coconut Rice

Makes 6–8 servings

Ideal slow cooker: 3-qt.

1½ cups uncooked long grain rice

2½ cups water

1 tsp. salt

6–8 oz. unsalted cashew halves, chopped coarsely

2 Tbsp. butter

7 oz. flaked coconut

1 tsp. curry powder

1. Combine rice, water, and salt in greased slow cooker. Cover and cook on low for 2 to 3 hours or until liquid is fully absorbed.

2. While rice cooks, sauté cashews in butter in a skillet until lightly browned. Stir in coconut and curry powder. Set aside.

3. When the rice is cooked, stir cashew coconut-curry mixture into rice mixture.

Herbed Rice

Makes 6 servings

Ideal slow cooker: 3½-qt.

3 chicken bouillon cubes

3 cups hot water

1½ cups uncooked long grain rice

¼ cup chopped fresh parsley

¼ cup sliced green onions

1 Tbsp. butter

1 tsp. dried rosemary

½ tsp. dried marjoram

½ cup sliced almonds (optional)

1. Stir together chicken bouillon cubes and water in slow cooker.

2. Add remaining ingredients, except almonds, in slow cooker.

3. Cover and cook on low 3½ to 4 hours or until rice is fully cooked. Toss with almonds, if desired, before serving.

NOTE

If you prefer, substitute 24 oz. (3 cups) fat-free low-sodium chicken broth for the bouillon cubes and water.

Peppered Corn on the Cob

Makes 5 servings

Ideal slow cooker: 5-qt.

6 Tbsp. butter, softened

4 garlic cloves, pressed

5 ears fresh corn, husks removed

1 tsp. freshly ground pepper

½ tsp. salt

15 fully cooked bacon slices

½ cup chicken broth

1 jalapeño pepper, minced

1. Combine butter and garlic in a small bowl. Rub garlic butter evenly over ears of corn. Sprinkle evenly with pepper and salt. Wrap each ear of corn with 3 bacon slices and secure with wooden picks. Place corn in slow cooker. Add broth and jalapeño.

2. Cover and cook on low 3 to 4 hours or until corn is tender. Remove bacon before serving, if desired.

Confetti Scalloped Corn

Makes 6–8 servings

Ideal slow cooker: 3- to 3½-qt.

2 eggs, beaten

I cup sour cream

¼ cup butter or margarine, melted

I small onion, finely chopped, or 2 Tbsp. dried chopped onion

I (11-oz.) can Mexican-style corn, drained

I (14-oz.) can cream-style corn

2–3 Tbsp. green jalapeño salsa, regular salsa, or chopped green chilies

I (8½-oz.) pkg. corn bread mix

6–8 slices bacon, cooked and crumbled (optional)

1. Combine all ingredients except bacon in a bowl. Pour into lightly greased slow cooker.

2. Cover and cook on high 2 to 2½ hours or until corn is set. Sprinkle with bacon, if desired.

Baked Corn

Makes 6 servings
Ideal slow cooker: 3- or 4-qt.

2 (14-oz.) cans cream-style corn

1½ cups milk

4 eggs, beaten

¼ cup butter, melted

2 Tbsp. sugar

2 Tbsp. all-purpose flour

1–1½ tsp. salt

¼ tsp. pepper

1. Combine all ingredients in greased slow cooker.

2. Cover and cook on low 4 hours or until a knife inserted in center comes out clean.

Apple-Walnut Squash

Makes 4 servings

Ideal slow cooker: 2- to 3-qt.

¼ cup water

2 small acorn squash

¼ cup firmly packed brown sugar

¼ cup butter, melted

3 Tbsp. apple juice

1½ tsp. ground cinnamon

¼ tsp. salt

1 cup walnuts, toasted

1 apple, chopped

1. Pour ¼ cup water into slow cooker.

2. Cut squash crosswise in half. Remove seeds. Place squash in slow cooker, cut sides up.

3. Combine brown sugar, butter, apple juice, cinnamon, and salt in a bowl. Spoon into squash.

4. Cover and cook on high 3 to 4 hours or until squash is tender.

5. Combine walnuts and chopped apple in a bowl. Add to center of squash and mix with sauce to serve.

6. Serve with a pork dish.

Orange Yams

Makes 6–8 servings

Ideal slow cooker: 3½-qt.

6–8 medium yams

2 apples, peeled if desired and thinly sliced

3 Tbsp. butter, melted

2 tsp. orange zest

I cup orange juice

2 Tbsp. cornstarch

½ cup packed brown sugar

I tsp. salt

Dash of ground cinnamon and/or nutmeg

Garnish: chopped pecans

1. Place yams and apples in slow cooker.

2. Stir in butter and orange zest.

3. Combine remaining ingredients except pecans in a small bowl. Pour over yams and apples.

4. Cover and cook on high 1 hour and then on low 2 hours or until apples are tender. Garnish, if desired.

Variation:

Substitute a 40-ounce can of yams or sweet potatoes or approximately 4 cups cubed butternut squash for the yams.

Apples 'n' Yams

Makes 8–10 servings

Ideal slow cooker: 4- to 5-qt.

6 apples, peeled and sliced

6 large yams or sweet potatoes, peeled and thinly sliced

1 Tbsp. lemon juice or lemonade

¼ cup apple juice

1 Tbsp. butter, melted

1. Toss sliced apples and yams in lemon juice in greased slow cooker.

2. Combine apple juice and butter in a 1-cup measure. Pour over apples and yams.

3. Cover and cook on high 4 hours or on low 6 hours.

TIP

This is a tasty vegetable dish to add to a meal for children. The apples smell wonderful while cooking and moistening the potatoes. It is also a well-rounded and easy way to serve sweet potatoes.

Calico Beans

Makes 12–15 servings

Ideal slow cooker: 4-qt.

1 lb. bacon

1 lb. ground beef

½ cup chopped onion

½ cup chopped celery

½ cup ketchup

1 Tbsp. prepared mustard

1 (16-oz.) can kidney beans, undrained

1 (16-oz.) can great northern beans, undrained

½ cup brown sugar

1 Tbsp. vinegar

1 (16-oz.) can butter beans, undrained

1 (28-oz.) can baked beans

1. Cut bacon into small pieces. Brown in a skillet. Drain.

2. Brown ground beef in skillet and drain, reserving drippings.

3. Sauté onion and celery in reserved drippings until soft.

4. Combine all ingredients in slow cooker.

5. Cover and cook on low 3 to 4 hours.

New Orleans Red Beans

Makes 6 servings

Ideal slow cooker: 3½-qt.

2 cups dried kidney beans

5 cups water

¼ lb. lean hot sausage, cut into small pieces

2 onions, chopped

2 garlic cloves, minced

1 tsp. salt

1. Sort and wash beans. Combine beans and 5 cups water in a saucepan and bring to a boil. Boil 2 minutes. Remove from heat. Soak 1 hour. Do not drain.

2. Brown sausage slowly in a nonstick skillet. Add onions, garlic, and salt and sauté until tender.

3. Combine all ingredients, including the bean water, in slow cooker.

4. Cover and cook on low 8 to 10 hours. During last 20 minutes of cooking, stir frequently and mash beans lightly with spoon to make desired consistency.

NOTE

Offer salsa as a condiment with this New Orleans–style dish.

"Stir-Fry" Veggies

Makes 8 servings

Ideal slow cooker: 6-qt.

1 (16-oz.) bag baby carrots

4 celery ribs, cut into chunks

1 medium onion, diced

1 (14½-oz.) can low-sodium Italian-style stewed tomatoes, undrained

½ tsp. dried basil

½ tsp. dried oregano

½ tsp. salt

1 large red or yellow bell pepper, diced

1 small head cabbage, chopped

1 lb. fresh broccoli, chopped

1. Combine carrots, celery, onion, tomatoes, basil, oregano, and salt in slow cooker.

2. Cover and cook on high 3 to 4 hours or on low 6 to 8 hours, stirring occasionally.

3. Stir in bell pepper, cabbage, and broccoli.

4. Cook on high 1 hour or on low 2 hours, stirring occasionally. You may need to add a little water if there is no liquid left on the veggies.

NOTE

Serve this as a side dish or as a main dish over hot cooked rice garnished with Parmesan cheese.

Scalloped Potatoes Supreme

Makes 4 servings

Ideal slow cooker: 4- to 5-qt.

4 medium potatoes, peeled and
sliced into rounds, *divided*

⅓ cup chopped onion

I Tbsp. all-purpose flour, *divided*

I tsp. salt, *divided*

⅛ tsp. pepper, *divided*

I cup diced cooked ham

I Tbsp. butter, cut into small pieces

1⅔ cups whole milk

I Tbsp. cornstarch

½ cup shredded sharp cheddar cheese

Garnish: chopped fresh chives

1. Arrange half the potatoes in greased slow cooker. Sprinkle with onion, 1½ teaspoons flour, ½ teaspoon salt, and a pinch of pepper.

2. Top with remaining potatoes and ham.

3. Sprinkle with remaining flour, salt, and pepper. Dot with butter.

4. Whisk together milk and cornstarch in a small bowl. Pour milk mixture down along one side of layers in slow cooker so as not to disturb seasonings and flour.

5. Cover and cook on low 4 to 5 hours, until potatoes are almost fork-tender. Top with cheese.

6. Increase heat to high and cook, uncovered, 15 to 30 minutes more, until cheese is melted and potatoes are tender. Garnish, if desired. Serve immediately.

Mashed Potatoes

Makes 4 servings

Ideal slow cooker: 3-qt.

4 medium potatoes

8 cups water

2⅔ cups milk

½ cup butter, melted

½ tsp. salt

Garnish: pepper, chopped fresh parsley

1. Peel potatoes. Place in a stockpot. Add 8 cups water to stockpot. Cover and cook on stovetop over medium heat until soft.

2. Check after about 20 minutes to make sure potatoes aren't cooking dry. If nearly dry, add another inch or so of water.

3. When potatoes are falling-apart soft, mash with potato masher or beat with handheld electric mixer.

4. While mashing potatoes, heat milk to scalding. Then add hot milk, butter, and salt to mashed potatoes, stirring in well.

5. Transfer potatoes to slow cooker a couple of hours before serving. Turn slow cooker to low. Stir occasionally. Garnish, if desired.

TIP

This recipe keeps you from mashing potatoes at the last minute.

Scalloped Taters

Makes 6–8 servings

Ideal slow cooker: 4-qt.

½ cup melted butter

¼ cup dried onion flakes

1 (16-oz.) pkg. frozen hash browns

1 (10¾-oz.) can cream of chicken soup

1½ cups milk

1 cup shredded cheddar cheese

⅛ tsp. black pepper

1 cup crushed cornflakes

Fresh parsley (optional)

1. Stir together butter, onions, potatoes, soup, milk, cheese, pepper, and ½ cup cornflakes. Pour into greased slow cooker. Top with remaining cornflakes.

2. Cover and cook on high 3 to 4 hours. Garnish, if desired.

Company Potatoes

Makes 6–8 servings

Ideal slow cooker: 3½- to 4-qt.

6 medium potatoes, cooked, cooled, and shredded

2 cups shredded cheddar cheese

⅓ cup finely chopped onion

¼ cup butter, melted

I tsp. salt

¼ tsp. pepper

1½–2 cups sour cream

Butter

1. Combine potatoes, cheese, onion, melted butter, salt, pepper, and sour cream in slow cooker. Dot with butter.

2. Cover and cook on low 4 hours.

NOTE

To prepare cooked potatoes for Step 1, first peel potatoes. Place whole potatoes in stockpot. Add at least 1 inch of water to stockpot. Cover. Cook on stovetop over medium heat until soft. Check frequently to make sure potatoes aren't cooking dry; add water if needed. Cool potatoes to room temperature. Then refrigerate 4 to 8 hours or until thoroughly chilled. Shred into slow cooker. Continue with Step 1 above.

Desserts and Drinks

Apple-Cranberry Crisp

Makes 8–10 servings

Ideal slow cooker: 4-qt.

3 cups chopped unpeeled apples

2 cups fresh cranberries

⅓ cup sugar

1½ cups uncooked regular or quick-cooking oats

½ cup packed brown sugar

⅓ cup all-purpose flour

⅓ cup chopped pecans

4 oz. (½ cup) butter, melted

Ice cream (optional)

1. Combine apples, cranberries, and sugar in greased slow cooker, mixing thoroughly to blend well.

2. Cover and cook on low 4 hours or until apples are soft.

3. While apple mixture cooks, stir remaining ingredients in a bowl until mixture is crumbly. Set aside.

4. When apples are done, sprinkle oat mixture over hot fruit.

5. Cook, uncovered, on low 30 to 45 minutes more, until topping begins to brown around edges. Serve warm with ice cream, if desired.

Caramel Apples

Makes 8–10 servings

Ideal slow cooker: 2-qt.

2 (14-oz.) bags of caramels

¼ cup water

8–10 medium apples

12–15 sticks, in case a few break

Granulated sugar in a dish

Waxed paper, lightly greased

1. Remove wrapping from caramels. Combine candies and water in slow cooker. Cover and cook on high 1 to 1½ hours, stirring every 5 minutes.

2. Meanwhile, wash and dry apples. Insert a stick into stem end of each apple.

3. Turn slow cooker to low. Dip apple into hot caramel, turning to coat entire surface.

4. Holding apple above cooker, scrape off excess accumulation of caramel from bottom of apple.

5. Dip bottom of caramel-coated apple in granulated sugar to keep it from sticking. Place apple on greased waxed paper to cool.

TIP

Top with crushed nuts, chocolate chips, sprinkles, or other desired toppings.

Baked Apples

Makes 4 servings

Ideal slow cooker: 3- or 4-qt.

4 unpeeled baking apples, cored

1 tsp. ground cinnamon

¼ cup brown sugar

4 Tbsp. butter

1. Place apples in slow cooker, making sure each is standing upright on the bottom.

2. Combine cinnamon and brown sugar in a small bowl. Stuff into apples.

3. Top each apple with 1 tablespoon butter.

4. Cover and cook on low 4 to 5 hours.

Serving suggestion:

Chop these apples to make a delicious topping for ice cream. They can also be served warm as a side dish or as a topping for waffles or pancakes.

Pumpkin-Pecan Pie

Makes 8–10 servings

Ideal slow cooker: 4- or 5-qt.

1 (14.1-oz.) pkg. refrigerated piecrusts

4 eggs

1 (16-oz.) can pumpkin

¾ cup sugar

½ cup dark corn syrup

1 tsp. cinnamon

¼ tsp. salt

1 cup pecans

Garnish: whipped cream

1. Press piecrusts into cold slow cooker, overlapping seams by ¼ inch. Tear off pieces so that dough fits partway up sides, pressing pieces together at all seams.

2. Beat eggs lightly in a large bowl. Stir in pumpkin, sugar, corn syrup, cinnamon, and salt.

3. Pour into slow cooker and arrange pecans over pumpkin mixture.

4. Cover and cook on high 1½ hours or until filling is set and a knife inserted in center comes out clean.

5. Serve in bowls and garnish, if desired.

Easy Autumn Cake

Makes 8 servings

Ideal slow cooker: 3½- or 4-qt.

2 (16-oz.) cans sliced apples, undrained
1 (18¼-oz.) pkg. spice cake mix
4 oz. (½ cup) butter, melted
½ cup chopped pecans

1. Spray inside of slow cooker with cooking spray.

2. Spoon apples and their juice into slow cooker, spreading evenly over bottom.

3. Sprinkle with dry cake mix. Pour melted butter over cake mix. Top with chopped pecans.

4. Cover and cook on low 3 to 5 hours or until a toothpick inserted into topping comes out clean.

5. Serve warm from slow cooker.

Gooey Chocolate Cake

Makes 8–12 servings

Ideal slow cooker: 4-qt.

I cup all-purpose flour

2 tsp. baking powder

2 Tbsp. butter

2 oz. semisweet chocolate
or ⅓ cup chocolate chips

I cup brown sugar, *divided*

3 Tbsp. plus ⅓ cup
Dutch-processed cocoa, *divided*

I Tbsp. vanilla extract

¼ tsp. salt

⅓ cup skim milk

I egg yolk

1½ cups hot water

Garnishes: whipped cream,
maraschino cherries with stems

1. Coat inside of slow cooker with cooking spray.

2. Combine flour and baking powder in a bowl. Set aside.

3. Melt butter and chocolate in microwave in a large microwave-safe mixing bowl. Stir well.

4. Whisk in ⅔ cup brown sugar, 3 tablespoons cocoa, vanilla, salt, milk, and egg yolk.

5. Add flour mixture and stir until thoroughly mixed. Pour batter into slow cooker and spread evenly.

6. Whisk together remaining ⅓ cup brown sugar, ⅓ cup cocoa, and 1½ cups hot water until sugar is dissolved. Pour over batter in slow cooker. Do not stir.

7. Cover and cook on high 1 to 2 hours. Cake will be very moist and floating on a layer of molten chocolate when it's done. It is done cooking when nearly all the cake is set and edges begin to pull away from sides of slow cooker.

8. Turn off slow cooker and remove lid, being careful not to let condensation from lid drip onto cake.

9. Let cool 25 minutes before cutting and spooning onto individual plates. Garnish, if desired.

Fudgy Peanut Butter Cake

Makes 4 servings

Ideal slow cooker: 2- or 3-qt.

¾ cup sugar, *divided*

½ cup flour

¾ tsp. baking powder

⅓ cup milk

¼ cup peanut butter

I Tbsp. vegetable oil

½ tsp. vanilla extract

2 Tbsp. dry cocoa powder

I cup boiling water

1. Butter or spray interior of slow cooker with cooking spray.

2. Mix ¼ cup sugar, flour, and baking powder together in a small bowl.

3. In a separate larger bowl, mix milk, peanut butter, oil, and vanilla together. Beat well.

4. Stir dry ingredients into milk-peanut butter mixture just until combined. Spread in buttered slow cooker.

5. In bowl, combine cocoa powder and remaining ½ cup sugar. Add water, stirring until well mixed. Pour slowly into slow cooker. Do not stir.

6. Cover. Cook on high 1½ hours, or until toothpick inserted in center of cake comes out clean.

Serving suggestion:

Serve warm with vanilla ice cream.

Apple-Caramel Dessert

Makes 7 servings

Ideal slow cooker: 3-qt.

½ cup apple juice

7 oz. caramel candies

1 tsp. vanilla extract

⅛ tsp. ground cardamom

½ tsp. ground cinnamon

⅓ cup creamy peanut butter

2 medium apples, peeled, cored, and cut into wedges

7 slices angel food cake

1 qt. vanilla ice cream

1. Combine apple juice, caramel candies, vanilla, and spices. Place in slow cooker.

2. Drop peanut butter, 1 teaspoon at a time, into slow cooker. Stir.

3. Add apple wedges.

4. Cover and cook on low 5 hours.

5. Stir well.

6. Cover and cook on low 1 hour more.

7. Serve ⅓ cup warm mixture over each slice of angel food cake and top with ice cream.

Lemon Pudding Cake

Makes 5–6 servings

Ideal slow cooker: 4-qt.

3 eggs, separated

1 tsp. grated lemon rind

¼ cup lemon juice

3 Tbsp. butter, melted

1½ cups milk

¾ cup sugar

¼ cup all-purpose flour

⅛ tsp. salt

1. Beat egg whites in a bowl until stiff peaks form. Set aside.

2. Beat egg yolks in a bowl. Blend in lemon rind, lemon juice, butter, and milk.

3. In a separate bowl, combine sugar, flour, and salt. Add to lemon mixture, beating until smooth.

4. Fold into beaten egg whites.

5. Spoon into slow cooker.

6. Cover and cook on high 2 to 3 hours.

7. Serve with a spoon from slow cooker.

Quick Apple Cobbler

Makes 8 servings

Ideal slow cooker: 4-qt.

½ cup butter, melted

I cup all-purpose flour

I cup sugar

2 tsp. baking powder

½ tsp. salt

½ tsp. ground cinnamon

I cup milk

4 cups chopped apples

1. Grease inside of slow cooker.

2. Place butter in slow cooker.

3. Combine flour, sugar, baking powder, salt, and cinnamon in a bowl. Stir in milk until smooth. Spoon into the cooker on top of the butter. Do not stir.

4. Spoon chopped apples evenly over batter. Do not stir.

5. Cover and cook on high 1½ to 2 hours or until a toothpick inserted into center of cake comes out clean. Serve warm with milk or ice cream, if desired.

Double-Berry Cobbler

Makes 6 servings

Ideal slow cooker: 5-qt.

1 cup all-purpose flour

1 ½ cups sugar, *divided*

1 tsp. baking powder

¼ tsp. salt

¼ tsp. ground cinnamon

¼ tsp. ground nutmeg

2 eggs, beaten

2 Tbsp. milk

2 Tbsp. vegetable oil

2 cups fresh or frozen blueberries

2 cups fresh or frozen blackberries

¾ cup water

1 tsp. grated orange rind

Whipped topping or ice cream (optional)

1. Combine flour, ¾ cup sugar, baking powder, salt, cinnamon, and nutmeg in a large bowl.

2. Combine eggs, milk, and oil in a separate bowl. Stir into dry ingredients until moistened.

3. Spread batter evenly over bottom of greased slow cooker.

4. Combine berries, ¾ cup water, orange rind, and remaining ¾ cup sugar in a saucepan. Bring to a boil. Remove from heat and pour over batter.

5. Cover and cook on high 2 to 2½ hours or until a toothpick inserted into cobbler comes out clean. Turn off slow cooker.

6. Uncover and let stand 30 minutes before serving. Spoon from slow cooker and serve with whipped topping or ice cream, if desired.

Strawberry-Rhubarb Parfaits

Makes 6–8 servings

Ideal slow cooker: 3-qt.

6 cups chopped rhubarb

1 cup sugar

1 cinnamon stick

½ cup white grape juice

2 cups sliced strawberries

1. Place rhubarb in slow cooker. Pour sugar over rhubarb. Add cinnamon stick and grape juice. Stir well.

2. Cover and cook on low 5 to 6 hours or until rhubarb is tender.

3. Stir in strawberries. Cover and cook 30 minutes more.

4. Remove cinnamon stick. Chill.

5. Serve over cake or ice cream.

Chocolate-Peanut Butter Cake

Makes 11 servings

Ideal slow cooker: 4-qt.

2 cups (half an 18.25-oz. pkg.) milk chocolate cake mix

½ cup water

¼ cup peanut butter

1 egg

2 egg whites

6 Tbsp. chopped walnuts

1. Combine all ingredients. Beat 2 minutes with electric mixer.

2. Pour into a greased and floured 3-pound shortening can. Place can in slow cooker.

3. Cover top of can with 8 paper towels.

4. Cover and cook on high 2 to 3 hours.

5. Cool 10 minutes. Run knife around edge and invert cake onto serving plate. Cool completely before slicing and serving.

Curried Fruit

Makes 8–10 servings

Ideal slow cooker: 3½-qt.

I can peaches, undrained

I can apricots, undrained

I can pears, undrained

I large can pineapple chunks, undrained

I can black cherries, undrained

½ cup firmly packed brown sugar

I tsp. curry powder

3–4 Tbsp. quick-cooking tapioca, depending upon how thickened you'd like the finished dish to be

Butter or margarine (optional)

1. Combine fruit in a bowl. Let stand for at least 2 hours, or up to 8, to allow flavors to blend. Drain. Place in slow cooker.

2. Add remaining ingredients except butter. Mix well. Dot with butter, if desired.

3. Cover and cook on low 8 to 10 hours. Serve warm or at room temperature.

Autumn Latte

Makes 6 servings

Ideal slow cooker: 3-qt.

4 cups 2% milk

1 ½ cups strong brewed coffee, decaf
or regular

½ cup pureed, cooked pumpkin or
canned pumpkin

2 Tbsp. sugar

2–4 Tbsp. dark brown sugar

1 Tbsp. vanilla extract

½ tsp. cinnamon

¼ tsp. ground cloves

¼ tsp. ground nutmeg

⅛ tsp. ground ginger

Pinch salt

Whipped cream (optional)

Ground cinnamon (optional)

Cinnamon sticks (optional)

1. Combine first 11 ingredients in slow cooker. Whisk until thoroughly combined.

2. Cover and cook on high 2 hours or until steaming hot. Whisk again.

3. Ladle into mugs. If desired, dollop with whipped cream, sprinkle with cinnamon, and serve with cinnamon stick stirrers.

Apple Honey Tea

Makes 6 servings

Ideal slow cooker: 1-qt.

1 (12-oz.) can frozen apple juice/cider concentrate

2 Tbsp. instant tea powder

1 Tbsp. honey

½ tsp. ground cinnamon

1. Reconstitute the apple juice/cider concentrate according to package directions. Pour into slow cooker. Add tea powder, honey, and cinnamon. Stir to blend.

2. Heat on low 1 to 2 hours.

Orange Spiced Cider

Makes 8 servings

Ideal slow cooker: 2- or 3-qt.

4 cups unsweetened apple juice

1 (12-oz.) can orange juice concentrate, thawed

½ cup water

1 Tbsp. red cinnamon candies

½ tsp. ground nutmeg

1 tsp. whole cloves

8 cinnamon sticks, 3–4 inches long (optional)

8 fresh orange slices (optional)

1. Combine first 5 ingredients in slow cooker.

2. Place cloves on a piece of cheesecloth. Tie with string to create a bag. Submerge bag in juices in slow cooker.

3. Cover and cook on low 2 to 3 hours or until cider is very hot.

4. Remove bag before serving. Stir cider.

5. If you wish, place a cinnamon stick, topped with an orange slice, in each cup. Pour in hot cider.

Serving suggestion:

If you are serving this to children, consider adding red hot candies instead of cinnamon sticks for a bit of fun and variety.

Hot Mulled Cider

Makes 8 servings

Ideal slow cooker: 3½-qt.

1 tsp. whole cloves
¼ cup brown sugar
2 qt. apple cider
1 cinnamon stick, 3 inches long
1 orange, sliced

1. Tie cloves in cheesecloth.

2. Combine all ingredients in slow cooker.

3. Cover and cook on low 3 to 6 hours. Remove cheesecloth before serving.

Spicy Hot Cider

Makes 16 servings

Ideal slow cooker: 4-qt.

I gallon cider
4 cinnamon sticks
2 Tbsp. ground allspice
½ cup brown sugar

1. Combine all ingredients in slow cooker.

2. Cover and cook on low 3 hours.

3. Remove cinnamon sticks before serving.

Spicy Autumn Punch

Makes 16 servings

Ideal slow cooker: 4-qt.

8 whole cloves

2 oranges

6 cups apple juice

1 cinnamon stick

$\frac{1}{4}$ tsp. ground nutmeg

3 Tbsp. lemon juice

$\frac{1}{4}$ cup honey

$2\frac{1}{4}$ cups pineapple juice

1. Press cloves into oranges. Bake at 325 to 350°F for 30 minutes.

2. Meanwhile, combine apple juice and cinnamon stick in slow cooker.

3. Cover and cook on high 1 hour.

4. Add remaining ingredients except oranges.

5. Cover and cook on low 2 to 3 hours. Add oranges at end, either whole or in quarters.

Delta Tea

Makes 6 cups

Ideal slow cooker: 3-qt. oval

1 (6-oz.) can frozen lemonade, thawed

5 cups water

1 tsp. vanilla extract

1 tsp. almond extract

1 Tbsp. instant tea mix

Garnishes: lemon slices and fresh mint

1. Combine all ingredients except garnishes in slow cooker.

2. Cover and cook on high 2 hours or until very hot.

3. Serve hot from the cooker, or chill and serve over ice. Garnish, if desired.

Wassail Punch

Makes 18 servings

Ideal slow cooker: 4-qt.

2 qt. apple cider

2 cups orange juice

2 cups pineapple juice

½ cup lemon juice

⅓–½ cup sugar, according to your taste preference

12 whole cloves

4 cinnamon sticks

1. Combine all ingredients in slow cooker. Mix well.

2. Cover and cook on low 2 to 3 hours.

3. Remove cloves and cinnamon sticks before serving.

Metric Equivalent Measurements

If you're accustomed to using metric measurements, I don't want you to be inconvenienced by the imperial measurements I use in this book.

Use this handy chart, too, to figure out the size of the slow cooker you'll need for each recipe.

Weight (Dry Ingredients)

1 oz		30 g
4 oz	¼ lb	120 g
8 oz	½ lb	240 g
12 oz	¾ lb	360 g
16 oz	1 lb	480 g
32 oz	2 lb	960 g

Slow Cooker Sizes

1-quart	0.96 l
2-quart	1.92 l
3-quart	2.88 l
4-quart	3.84 l
5-quart	4.80 l
6-quart	5.76 l
7-quart	6.72 l
8-quart	7.68 l

Volume (Liquid Ingredients)

½ tsp.		2 ml
1 tsp.		5 ml
1 Tbsp.	½ fl oz	15 ml
2 Tbsp.	1 fl oz	30 ml
¼ cup	2 fl oz	60 ml
⅓ cup	3 fl oz	80 ml
½ cup	4 fl oz	120 ml
⅔ cup	5 fl oz	160 ml
¾ cup	6 fl oz	180 ml
1 cup	8 fl oz	240 ml
1 pt	16 fl oz	480 ml
1 qt	32 fl oz	960 ml

Length

¼ in	6 mm
½ in	13 mm
¾ in	19 mm
1 in	25 mm
6 in	15 cm
12 in	30 cm

Recipe and Ingredient Index

About the Author

Hope Comerford is a mom, wife, elementary music teacher, blogger, recipe developer, public speaker, ALM Zone Fitness Motivator, Young Living Essential Oils essential oil enthusiast/educator, and published author. In 2013, she was diagnosed with a severe gluten intolerance and since then has spent many hours creating easy, practical, and delicious gluten-free recipes that can be enjoyed by both those who are affected by gluten and those who are not.

Growing up, Hope spent many hours in the kitchen with her Meme (grandmother), and her love for cooking grew from there. While working on her master's degree when her daughter was young, Hope turned to her slow cookers for some salvation and sanity. It was from there she began truly experimenting with recipes and quickly learned she had the ability to get a little more creative in the kitchen and develop her own recipes.

In 2010, Hope started her blog, *A Busy Mom's Slow Cooker Adventures*, to simply share the recipes she was making with her family and friends. She never imagined people all over the world would begin visiting her page and sharing her recipes with others as well. In 2013, Hope self-published her first cookbook, *Slow Cooker Recipes 10 Ingredients or Less and Gluten-Free*, and then later wrote *The Gluten-Free Slow Cooker*.

Hope is thrilled to be working with Fix-It and Forget-It and to be representing such an iconic line of cookbooks. She is excited to bring her creativity to the Fix-It and Forget-It brand. Through Fix-It and Forget-It, Hope has written many books, including *Fix-It and Forget-It Lazy & Slow*, *Fix-It and Forget-It Healthy Slow Cooker Cookbook*, *Fix-It and Forget-It Favorite Slow Cooker Recipes for Mom*, *Fix-It and Forget-It Favorite Slow Cooker Recipes for Dad*, and *Fix-It and Forget-It Instant Pot Cookbook*. Hope lives in the city of Clinton Township, Michigan, near Metro Detroit, and is a Michigan native. She has been happily married to her husband and best friend, Justin, since 2008. Together they have two children, Ella and Gavin, who are her motivation, inspiration, and heart. In her spare time, Hope enjoys traveling, singing, cooking, reading books, spending time with friends and family, and relaxing.